# BASIL LANNEAU GILDERSLEEVE

*AJP* Monographs in Classical Philology

This new series of publications of the *American Journal of Philology* is intended to meet a need in the broad field of classical studies. Its primary purpose is to publish and to encourage the publication of significant work that is too long to appear in article form and too short for a conventional book (that is, manuscripts of between one hundred and two hundred pages). The series is also open to longer monographs in the fields covered by the journal—Greek and Roman literature, textual criticism, classical linguistics, ancient philosophy, and Greek and Latin epigraphy.

Diskin Clay, Editor, *American Journal of Philology*

1. *Basil Lanneau Gildersleeve: An American Classicist*, edited by Ward W. Briggs, Jr., and Herbert W. Benario

**Basil Lanneau Gildersleeve (1831–1924)**

Courtesy of Mrs. Katharine L. Weems. Photo by Rick Stafford.

# *BASIL LANNEAU GILDERSLEEVE*

# An American Classicist

Ward W. Briggs, Jr.
Herbert W. Benario
*Editors*

THE JOHNS HOPKINS UNIVERSITY PRESS
Baltimore and London

© 1986 The Johns Hopkins University Press
All rights reserved
Printed in the United States of America

The Johns Hopkins University Press
701 West 40th Street
Baltimore, Maryland 21211

The Johns Hopkins Press Ltd.
London

*The paper used in this publication meets the minimum requirements of American National Standard for Information Sciences—Permanence of Paper for Printed Library Materials, ANSI Z39.48-1984.* ∞™

Library of Congress Cataloging-in-Publication Data

Main entry under title:
Basil Lanneau Gildersleeve : an American classicist.

  Chiefly papers presented at a session of the fall
1982 meeting of the Southern Section of the Classical
Association of the Middle West and South in Charlottes-
ville, Va.
  "Select bibliography of Basil L. Gildersleeve": p.
  Includes index.
  1. Gildersleeve, Basil L. (Basil Lanneau), 1831-1924
—Congresses.   2. Classicists—United States—Biography
—Congresses.   3. Classical philology—Study and
teaching—United States—Congresses.   I. Briggs, Ward W.
II. Benario, Herbert W.   III. Classical Association of
the Middle West and South.
PA85.G48B37   1985      880′.092′4[B]85-25619
ISBN 0-8018-3117-2

*The printer's device on the cover of this book is that of Aldus Manutius. It was selected from among the ones especially created in stained glass for the Hutzler Undergraduate Reading Room on the Homewood campus of The Johns Hopkins University.*

# CONTRIBUTORS

Herbert W. Benario is Professor of Classics at Emory University. He has edited *Tacitus Annals 11 and 12*.

Ward W. Briggs, Jr., is Professor of Classics at the University of South Carolina. He has written on Virgil and is currently editing Gildersleeve's letters.

Robert L. Fowler is Assistant Professor of Classics at the University of Waterloo, Ontario, Canada. He is the author of the forthcoming *The Nature of Early Greek Lyric*.

Deborah Reeves Hopkins teaches Latin and French at Ashley Hall in Charleston, South Carolina. She is completing research on women in Pompeii.

George A. Kennedy is Paddison Professor of Classics at the University of North Carolina. He is the author of six books dealing with the history of rhetoric in the classical and later periods.

E. Christian Kopff is Associate Professor of Classics at the University of Colorado at Boulder. He is the author of a critical edition of Euripides' *Bacchae*.

Stephen Newmyer is Professor of Classics at Duquesne University. He has written on Statius and is editor of the *Biographical Dictionary of North American Classicists*.

Seth L. Schein is Professor of Classical Literature at the University of California at Santa Cruz. He has written *The Mortal Hero: An Introduction to Homer's Iliad* and *The Iambic Trimeter in Aeschylus and Sophocles: A Study in Metrical Form*.

John Vaio is Associate Professor of Classics at the University of Illinois at Chicago. He has written on Aristophanes and Babrius and is currently preparing a critical edition of the latter's *Mythiambi*.

# CONTENTS

# PREFACE

Seven of these papers were delivered at a session commemorating Basil Lanneau Gildersleeve at the Fall 1982 meeting of the Southern Section of The Classical Association of the Middle West and South in Charlottesville, Virginia. The date was November 5; we therefore missed by one year and less than a fortnight precise celebration of the 150th anniversary of the man generally regarded as this country's greatest classical scholar. It was a welcome opportunity to recall some aspects of his life and labors on the campus of Mr. Jefferson's university, which gave Gildersleeve his first academic appointment.

With a slight exception these papers are printed in the order of their delivery. George Kennedy's tribute has been added to complete the picture: three essays are biographical; three treat the major aspects of his career as teacher, grammarian, and editor; and two treat his tastes in classical literature and his uniquely American literary style. The session was a lively and stimulating one; we hope that some sense of the sympathy and excitement that pervaded the hall will survive here.

When publication of these papers became possible, we could not omit the opportunity of making available to the scholarly world Robert L. Fowler's report of his examination of the Gildersleeve archive in the library of the Johns Hopkins University. This appears as the second part of the volume.

Professor Benario originally conceived of the session, invited the participants, and presided over the program. After he had arranged for the publication of the present volume and done preliminary editing of the papers, commitments in Germany for the summer of 1984 and Rome for the school year 1984-5 obliged him to put the project in the hands of Professor Briggs, who thoroughly edited all the papers, prepared the manuscript for computer typesetting, and saw the book through the press.

Since this is the first book-length work devoted to Gildersleeve's life and career, such editing as has been done reflects the desire to put as many facts and resources (by the addition of notes) before those who have more than a passing interest in the subject, while keeping the essential character of the orally delivered papers. To avoid constant lengthy and repetitious references to Gildersleeve's own works, a select bibliography gives abbreviated references.

One pleasant duty remains, that of thanking all of our colleagues who participated with their learning and humor in this tribute and for their help in this later stage of publication. Professor Diskin Clay, editor of the *American Journal of Philology*, deserves no less gratitude for his constant interest in the project and his efforts in having the papers appear in a volume that marks the beginning of a new venture for the journal that Gildersleeve himself founded more than a century ago. *Utinam magister ipse de campis Elysiis coeptis nostris faveat!*

HERBERT W. BENARIO
WARD W. BRIGGS, JR.

# BASIL LANNEAU GILDERSLEEVE: THE CHARLESTON BACKGROUND

Deborah Reeves Hopkins

Basil Lanneau Gildersleeve established his allegiance unequivocally when he stated, "First a Charlestonian, I was next a Carolinian."[1] He was born in that city October 23, 1831, in the gracious house at #9 Pitt Street, the home of his Lanneau grandparents. In an autobiographic article in 1891, Gildersleeve expressed his feelings about his early Charleston upbringing and summarized his fourteen years there as the most formative of his life.

> I was proud of my native city; considered St. Michael's "one of the finest churches in the country, sir," — if not the finest; and believed in my heart of hearts that there was no more spacious promenade than the Battery — which I used to pace with a certain religious exaltation — no grander houses than the old family mansions, no nobler street than Meeting Street. I knew every nook and corner of the town, kept a map of Charleston in my room long after I had left the "confluence of the Ashley and Cooper Rivers,"[2] and would not suffer the memory of Amen Street and Zigzag Alley to perish.[3]

Gildersleeve termed the old Huguenot names "aristocratic music" in his ear, and he emphatically repeated, "I was a Charlestonian first, Carolinian next, and then a southerner — on my mother's side a southerner beyond dispute."[4]

Certainly Gildersleeve was proud of his home city and of his family there. Paul Shorey said that as Oliver Wendell Holmes would have it, he chose his ancestry wisely.[5] His mother, Emma Louisa Lanneau, was the daughter of Basile La Noue, who had arrived in Charleston in 1755 in one of the shiploads of French expelled by the British from Acadia.[6] Basile was aided by one of the most illustrious of Charleston's citizens, Henry Laurens, the American Revolutionary statesman. With the help of Laurens, he became apprenticed as a tanner. Later, when established and prospering, Basile returned to Acadia for other members of his family, and by his grandson's time, the flourishing Americanized Lanneau cousins formed somewhat of a family compound, lining Pitt Street with their comfortable dwellings, which are still features of Charleston's proud architectural heritage.

These Lanneaus participated in the life of the city as prominent merchants, bankers, legislators, and members of select social organizations.[7] The family members showed a definite propensity for Christian endeavors. Gildersleeve could count among his relations the Reverend John F. Lanneau, who served long as a missionary to Jerusalem; Basil Edward Lanneau, for years Hebrew tutor in a theological seminary at Columbia, then professor at Oakland College in Mississippi;[8] and professor John Lanneau of Wake Forest University, who was his contemporary.[9] His sister responded to the correlative trend of religion and linguistics in the family line by marrying the Reverend Henry Pratt, who was a missionary in South America and Mexico, and who translated the Bible into Spanish.[10] Gildersleeve's boyhood enthusiasm for the Mexican War[11] could have resulted from Pratt's travels, and when, in the latter stages of the Civil War, he entertained the idea of fleeing to South America after the fall of the Confederacy,[12] he might have thought the Pratts would provide refuge.

Of his mother's participation in the family's prevalent religiosity, Gildersleeve said, "My mother was a loving woman of quick sensibilities, who had a heart full of true religion and a head free from theology, true or false; but her creed was that of her husband, and he was a theologian in grain and a doughty controversialist."[13]

This doughty controversialist, the Reverend Benjamin Gildersleeve, appears to have been the single most important person in Basil Gildersleeve's life. Basil saw his own life as oriented around the school and the printing office, and his father had been mentor and master in both. In his own words, his early training was singular:

> After I left the nursery, until I was between twelve and thirteen, my father was my only teacher. My lessons were heard at odd hours, often when my father was tired from work; and hard was the work that would tire that heroic soul. . . . It was, as I remember it, a very tumultuous affair, that earliest education of mine. I could read when I was between three and four years of age, and I signalized the completion of my fifth year by reading the Bible from cover to cover. Needless to say, the reading was not with the understanding.[14]

Looking back on his attainments, Gildersleeve self-effacingly commented, "It is astonishing how much enjoyment one can get out of a language that one understands imperfectly."[15] Among the languages of which he had that enjoyable but imperfect understanding in his early youth were Latin, Greek, French, German, and Spanish.[16]

The elder Gildersleeve would not allow Basil to read "immoral" Shakespeare, as he put it, but the young boy could sneak the plays and Scott's Waverly novels from an "ungodly great-uncle," adding, "In his old age, my father became a novel-reader himself, but I never confessed my sin to him."[17] In another place, he adds, "My father, however, was a northern man, and that flaw in my title made me perhaps more tenacious of my nativity. But most of my southern kindred admitted that, for a northerner, he was a passably good southerner."[18] His father's favorite verse of the Psalms was "Blessed be the Lord my strength, which teacheth my hands to war and my fingers to fight. . . ."[19] Basil gained no slight inheritance from his father in this respect, for he fought many causes as bravely and tenaciously from his editor's table as from the saddle of a horse.[20]

Struggling and fighting was a part of the Gildersleeve family history. His grandfather Finch was active in the Huntington, New York, "Liberty Boys" and served with a regiment at Valley Forge under George Washington.[21] His father, Benjamin, was determined to achieve an education, and he made his own opportunities, despite obstacles. He went out to plow with a Latin grammar in his pocket. He molded his own training with that discipline which molded his son's, and which his son implemented in his own role as teacher. He took himself to Middlebury College, Vermont, then Hopewell Seminary in Athens, Georgia, then to Princeton Seminary, then he returned to Georgia. While there, he began the first in a long series of religious publications. After personal and professional disappointments, he was constrained to set out on a pilgrimage over the South in an effort to try to obtain funds to offset a financial crisis.[22] In the course of his travels, he crossed paths with Roman Catholic Bishop John England, church and education pioneer, for whom the Bishop England High School in Charleston is named. He crossed swords as well; their subsequent controversy in Charleston over the Old School and the New School thought was to take on the appearance of a cause célèbre. Gildersleeve recalled his father's "battle royal with Bishop England. Then for long months the air was resonant with the shouts of 'Old School' and 'New School,' and in this turmoil, my father's trumpet gave no uncertain sound."[23]

The argument of Old School-New School, which crystallized over the issue of whether evangelization should be carried on to slaves as well as to free men, was evidence of the church's participation in current thought on the eve of the American Civil War. Gildersleeve says that his father "was an ardent nullifier, and he had no misgivings on the great question of questions, for he had left his northern home before domestic slavery had ceased to exist in the upper tier of states."[24] If any question might remain as to why a son of a "Son of Liberty" would become an ardent Nullifier and the father of a defender of slavery, there is Gildersleeve's comment that "West Point made fewer converts to this side and to that than did . . . the Southern wives of Northern husbands."[25]

Just as Gildersleeve spoke an eloquent and rational defense of the South in the Civil War in his essays, "The Creed of the Old South" and "A Southerner in the Peloponnesian War,"[26] so in his scholarly publications he revealed the scars of the lost cause. In his introduction to Pindar, he argued that "it was no discredit to Pindar that he went honestly with his state in the struggle. . . . The Greece that came out of the Persian War was a very different thing from the cantons that ranged themselves on this side and that of a quarrel which, we may be sure, bore another aspect to those who stood aloof from it than it wears in the eyes of moderns, who have learned to be Hellenic patriots."[27] This was the Gildersleeve who stirred resentment among his professional colleagues, who would not surrender an opening for another word on behalf of his cause. Any opportunity for reminiscence of the Southern experience in the war was for Gildersleeve a partisan act his life long.

His father had arrived in Charleston in 1826 at a time when racial, class, and Mason-Dixon lines were being drawn taut. The considerable literary talent cultivated in her young men was turned toward expressing fire-eater thought. The humanistic momentum of the eighteenth century was checked, and as Gildersleeve is quoted as having remarked to an historian-friend, "the South Carolina mind after 1832 became a foetus in a bottle."[28] That year not only saw the Nat Turner slave rebellion, but also bounds tariff conflicts, the Missouri debates, local slave rebellions, and the Nullification crisis, as well as other issues of North-South tension. As Gildersleeve expressed it, most Southerners believed that they were fighting for the cause of civil liberty and not the cause of human slavery.[29] The biographer of William Gilmore Simms, W. P. Trent, had written in 1891 that such a view neglected the fact that it was human slavery which largely determined the nature of a Southerner's ideas of civil liberty.[30]

The Charleston into which Basil Lanneau Gildersleeve was born was the literary center of the South. This "Boston of the South"[31] is set amid steamy low-country marshes, washed by rich estuaries, and draped with Spanish moss; the composite effect attaches something sensual and primeval to the soul of every son and daughter. Gildersleeve mentions Morris Island several times in his writing, a place once a geographical feature just outside of Charleston harbor. Now it has washed away along with the bones of black Union soldiers who perished in their bitter and unsuccessful onslaught against the Confederate Fort Wagner there, in the battle that claimed friends of Gildersleeve and which prompted his comparison of Morris Island to Sphacteria.[32]

There was a uniqueness, an old-world look to the city, which historian George Rogers has recently called an "air of self-conscious individuality such as aged men wear,"[33] a description, one is tempted to gamble, that would have appealed to Gildersleeve. Along those narrow streets, men like Francis Marion and Charles Cotesworth Pinckney and Christopher Gadsden—and Basil La Noue—had walked, and along them their descendants walked. Historical fancies seemed real; romantic novels by Sir Walter Scott formed the pleasure reading, and regional heroes were likened to Roman exemplars.

But there were contemporary writers—Charleston published the best of the early Southern magazines[34]—led by William Gilmore Simms, Henry Timrod, the Poet Laureate of the Confederacy, and Paul Hamilton Hayne. Hayne and Timrod were slightly older than Gildersleeve, but he may have attended Christopher Coates' Classical School with them[35] before entering Charleston College (now the College of Charleston) as a boy of fourteen,[36] and upon his frequent returns to the city after receiving his German degree, he often joined these men at their gatherings at Russell's Book Shop on King Street, where Simms presided over the group.[37] All these men revered the culture of which they were exponents. They regarded their society as God's most favored. For Southern whites, their culture, as historian Samuel S. Hill has said, "to a greater degree than any other, approximates the ideals the Almighty has in mind for mankind everywhere."[38] Hayne, one of their number, claimed that his generation "looked upon literature as the choice recreation of gentlemen, as something fair and good, to be courted in a dainty, amateur fashion, and illustrated by *apropos* quotations from Lucretius, Virgil, or Horace."[39]

These men were poets first who enlisted their talents in the service of the Great Cause. In the ensemble besides Gildersleeve was another recent graduate of Göttingen, David Ramsay, the grandson of the Revolutionary War historian, who was destined to lose his life in the battle at Fort Wagner.[40] The loss of childhood Charleston friends because of the war was a great weight of sadness to Gildersleeve, as he often testified in print.[41]

The experience of belonging to Charleston's inner social circle (or one of Charleston's inner social circles) was not the same for all these men, however. William Gilmore Simms himself seems to have never really belonged, but one of his figures could have been a caricature of Gildersleeve's Lanneau relatives; witness Madame Agnes-Theresa Girardin: "She, a gaunt, colorless embodiment of family pride, walked down King Street like a social barometer, rising and falling, stiffening and unbending, according to the blueness of the blood of the persons she meets."[42] Basil Lanneau Gildersleeve had belonged to those families who claimed Charleston with rights of longevity and position. With friends who became poets and authors and an uncle an artist,[43] Gildersleeve's sensibilities were bound with his Charleston roots to lie within her intellectual and aesthetic disposition; accompanying this, it was his father, the minister and editor, who provided material for the boy's ideas and who directed his way.

He was a Southerner and thoroughly identified with the South. He owned that "I have shared the fortunes of the land in which my lot was cast, and in my time have shared its prejudices and its defiant attitude."[44] He combined the elements that blended to make a religion of the Lost Cause, a spiritual belief in a culture. He said about his life, "I see that all that came after lay implicit in that first period [the childhood spent in Charleston]. . . . I was made to recognize the duty of work by the unyielding pressure of the creed in which I was brought up."[45] This deep vein of local identification was matched and grew alongside its companion search for knowledge and truth, which is the key to the rest of the quotation, "That creed, it is true, seemed at times to have lost its hold, but the principle remained under every change of form. A professional ideal is as unrelenting as the Westminster Catechism."[46] This professional ideal is the proof, the lasting remembrance of the man who was a Charlestonian first.

# NOTES

[1]B. L. Gildersleeve, "Formative Influences," *Forum* X (February 1891) 608.

[2]Charlestonians are wont rather immodestly to point out that the Atlantic Ocean begins at the "confluence of the Ashley and Cooper Rivers."

[3]"Formative Influences," 607-8.

[4]Ibid., 608.

[5]Paul Shorey, "Basil Lanneau Gildersleeve—1831-1924; the Dean of American Scholars and Arch-Apostle of the Classics—His Career of Ninety-Three Years," *New York Times*, January 27, 1924, p. iv, col. 3.

[6]See Chapman J. Milling, *Exile Without an End* (Columbia, SC 1943) 58-60.

[7]*Charleston City Directories* (Charleston, SC 1807- ).

[8]Rev. George Howe, *History of the Presbyterian Church in South Carolina* (Columbia 1870) I, 303.

[9]Edward McCrady, *South Carolina under the Royal Government* (New York 1899) 328n.

[10]David Duncan Wallace, *History of South Carolina* (New York 1934) IV, 260-61.

[11]B. L. Gildersleeve, "The Creed of the Old South," *Atlantic Monthly* 69 (1892) 84 (=*Gildersleeve 5*, 43).

[12]"Formative Influences," 616.

[13]Ibid., 609.

[14]Ibid., 610-11.

[15]Ibid., 611.

[16]"French I picked up after a fashion . . . before I was fourteen. . . . Of German I knew only a few words . . . of Spanish I had learned something in a private class at Richmond" (Ibid., 611, 614).

[17]Ibid., 612.

[18]Ibid., 608.

[19]Ibid., 609. The verse is Ps. 144.1.

[20]Diana Lynn Walzel, "Basil Lanneau Gildersleeve: Classical Scholar," *Virginia Cavalcade* XXV (Winter 1976) 110-17. Ms. Walzel points out the combatant persona of Gildersleeve in a valuable and well-illustrated article. However, on page 116, she interprets Gildersleeve's statement that "the roots go back to the first fourteen years" as bearing on his years in Charlottesville, when, in fact, it is fairly obvious that he was speaking of his childhood of fourteen years in Charleston. He had said that in several places. The duration of his tenure in Charlottesville was twenty years, 1856-1876.

[21]W. H. Gildersleeve, *Gildersleeve Pioneers* (Rutland, VT 1941) 240-42.

[22]Ibid., 242-49.

[23]"Formative Influences," 609. Benjamin Gildersleeve ultimately affirmed the assertion that the religious instruction of the Negroes was "The Great Duty, and in the truest and best sense, THE FIXED, THE SETTLED POLICY OF THE SOUTH." *Proceedings of the Meeting in Charleston, South Carolina, May 13–15, 1845, on the Religious Instruction of the Negroes* (Charleston 1845) 72.

[24]"Formative Influences," 608.

[25]"The Creed of the Old South," 83 (=*Gildersleeve 5*, 37).

[26]"A Southerner in the Peloponnesian War," *Atlantic Monthly* 80 (1897) 330-42. Both are reprinted in *The Creed of the Old South* (Baltimore 1915)(=*Gildersleeve 5*).

[27]*Gildersleeve, 1*, 16.

[28]Wallace (note 10 above) II, 453.

[29]"The Creed of the Old South," 87 (=*Gildersleeve 5*, 51).

[30]William P. Trent, *William Gilmore Simms* (1892; reprint, New York 1969) 254.

[31]Ibid., 23.

[32]"A Southerner in the Peloponnesian War," 335 (=*Gildersleeve 5*, 74).

[33]George C. Rogers, *Charleston in the Age of the Pinckneys* (Norman, OK 1969) 28.

[34]Ibid., 157.

[35]R. S. Moore, *A Man of Letters in the Nineteenth Century South* (Baton Rouge and London 1982) 5, 146, n. 3.

[36]"Formative Influences" (note 1 above) 613.

[37]Trent (note 31 above) 228-29, n. 254; M. C. S. Oliphant et al., *The Letters of William Gilmore Simms* (Columbia, SC 1952) I, cxxxvi.

[38]C. R. Wilson, *Baptized in Blood: The Religion of the Lost Cause* (Athens, GA 1980) 7.

[39]Trent (note 31 above) 25.

[40]E. Milby Burton, *The Siege of Charleston 1861–1865* (Columbia, SC 1970) 163; Trent (note 31 above) 229.

[41]"The Creed of the Old South," 79 (=*Gildersleeve 5*, 26).

[42]Drawn from William Gilmore Simms, *The Golden Christmas* (Charleston, SC 1852) 15–27.

[43]*The Chicora*, July 30, 1842.

[44]"Formative Influences," 609.

[45]Ibid., 612.

[46]Ibid., 612–13.

# BASIL L. GILDERSLEEVE AT THE UNIVERSITY OF VIRGINIA

Ward W. Briggs, Jr.

My topic is one to which Gildersleeve himself did not devote much autobiographical writing. Information is available, but much of the biographical rubbish that finds its way into self-serving university histories and old-boy memoirs must be judged severely. Moreover, in the case of a legendary figure like Gildersleeve, a trove of anecdotes accompanies his famous career. These I shall indulge myself in sparsely, not trying to be encyclopedic, but rather to clear up points about which misinformation has circulated.[1]

Gildersleeve returned home to Richmond in 1853 from three years of the finest classical education a man could receive on this planet. He returned with the examples and methods of his masters, Böckh, Ritschl, Schneidewin, and Franz,[2] and he returned with a doctorate from Göttingen passed with the highest honors. But he also returned with few prospects, an offer tendered from his alma mater, Princeton, being in his words, "so far inferior to what I, a conceited youngster, deemed my due as a Ph.D. with high honours from a German university, that the negotiations were broken off with some show of anger on both sides."[3] So for three years he pursued the dream first inculcated in him by his years of friendship with the editor of the *Southern Literary Messenger*, John R. Thompson,[4] his association with the loosely knit group of literati who gathered about the figure of William Gilmore Simms in Charleston, and the figure of Edgar Allan Poe, whom he had seen and heard in Richmond in 1849. These personalities unquestionably made the literary (as opposed to the academic) life highly attractive to Gildersleeve, and he responded with numerous short reviews for the *Messenger* and longer ones for the *Quarterly Review of the Methodist Episcopal Church, South*. He also completed a draft of the novel he started before leaving for Germany, the picaresque adventures of Alfred Thistledown, Esq. Ultimately he was reduced, in his words, to tasting "the salt bread of a tutorship with a private family"[5] on a plantation in the low country of South Carolina. For all that time he said that his ambition was "to be a poet, or failing that, a man of letters."[6] But finally, in 1856, the Professorship of Greek was created at the University of Virginia and was offered to Gildersleeve and to none other, probably through the efforts of Dr. Socrates Maupin,[7] who first employed Gildersleeve as a teacher in his school following his graduation from Princeton in 1849, and who, as Chairman of the Faculty in 1854 (he was Chairman of the Chemistry Department in 1855), undoubtedly had the power to secure the appointment for his young friend, who was in any case the Virginia native best qualified for the job. Thus, in 1856, in Gildersleeve's words, "I renounced literature as a profession and betook myself to teaching."[8]

Although Gildersleeve surely was to have a job at the leading Southern university, the situation of his early years in Charlottesville brought disappointments to endure as well as traditions to uphold.

The first Classics professor—indeed, the first of Jefferson's faculty to arrive on campus—was George Long, a fellow of Trinity College, Cambridge.[9] Then under the influence of Barthold Georg Niebuhr,[10] Long had given, in the words of Herbert B. Adams, "a character and a standard to the classical department which it has never lost. He represented history in connection with the classics and certainly ancient history never had a more scholarly representative upon American shores."[11] Long resigned in 1828 to become the first Professor of Greek at the new University of London. Long, who "fixed the standard of requirement of his classes at a higher point than was then known in this country,"[12] suggested as his successor his student, Gessner Harrison, a recent medical graduate of the University, who, at the age of only 21, began to teach what and how he had been taught by Long. In 1833, Long sent Harrison the first part of Bopp's *Comparative Grammar*, and by 1839 Harrison had published an outline of his lectures that would form the basis of the *Latin Grammar* he published in 1852.[13] This is all the more remarkable, for it is said that the Chair of Ancient Languages (Hebrew, Latin, Greek) at the time (1845–1855) was as taxing as any two in the University, and that students needed "as much application to win its diploma as to graduate in Moral Philosophy, Natural Philosophy, and Chemistry combined."[14] In addition, Harrison was extremely popular. John A. Broadus recalls, "Many remembered as an epoch in their lives the views of History and the enthusiasm for this study which they derived from Dr. Harrison."[15] In consequence, the number of students enrolled in the School of Ancient Languages, which in 1843 had been only 33, was 259 by 1855–1856. Further, Harrison performed many other ordinary duties on the campus and was elected chairman of the faculty five times. In 1851 he complained that the correction of exercises alone gave him no time for study or publication, particularly with no assistant to help him.[16] The two aides provided later were of so little help in relieving the problem that on May 26, 1856, the Board of Visitors voted to divide the professorship into a Chair of Latin and a Chair of Greek and Hebrew. Harrison was given his choice; he chose Latin and managed the then handsome salary of $1000 a year plus all the fees accruable from his classes (at $25 per student), much to the vocal irritation of his colleagues.

Here then was the scene Gildersleeve entered upon: Harrison was the shogun of Ancient Languages and a power at the University if for no other reason than his almost thirty years of active service. Embittered and, in the current phrase, "burnt-out" by the excessive work his own popularity had caused, deprived originally of the medical career he had trained for, and facing the enmity of his colleagues over his huge salary, he now, at 49, with years of the historical and comparatist method of the American university behind him, was confronted by the European-trained Gildersleeve, 24 years old and full of the methods and models of his German education.

What was Gildersleeve's response to his new job? It can easily be imagined from the following, taken from his essay "University Work in America," originally published in 1879:[17]

> Let us imagine a young man fresh from the best German schools. Such a supposition would have been construed as a personal allusion twenty-five years ago; it is hardly more definite now than to suppose a graduate of Harvard or Yale. Our young friend begins his novitiate either as a tutor in one of our large universities, or as a professor in some half-endowed college. The transition is one of the most painful that can be imagined. Even the return of the mythical good American from the Elysian Fields of Paris could scarcely be less distressing than the descent of the enthusiastic student from the academic heights of German university life to the unromantic levels of the American classroom. If our hero had spent a *semester* or more at a minor university, or followed the exercises of a *gymnasium* for a few months, all feeling of exaltation might have worn off and the fall might have been broken. But he comes from the best in quality and the richest in resource to our average. In the meagrely furnished library he misses his favorite books, or rather books which by frequent citation he seems to know; in the reading-room he cannot find the journals so familiar to eye and ear. He has no one who will suffer him to talk about the themes of his personal research or even the absorbing topic of his doctor-dissertation, because there is no one who has a like attention to exact of him in return. His duties are eminently distasteful. Instead of following the history of a construction, chasing an etymon through a score of lan-

guages, getting at the source of an historian, analysing the style of an
orator, he has to listen to translations of Xenophon's Anabasis, to correct
exercises in which Darius and Parysatis continue to have two sons in all
the moods and tenses, and, what is worst of all, he is often waked up out
of his learned dreams to find that the irregular Greek verbs, which he
once fancied he knew well enough, are to be an object of steady contem-
plation for the rest of his natural life, and that with all his gettings he has
still no end of work to do in the mechanical mastery, so to speak, of the
language to which he has devoted himself. The situation is grim, and
there is little help from without. Sometimes he is utterly alone. Sometimes
the traditions of the college or university do not favor easy intercourse
between the principal and subordinate teachers. But even when the older
colleague is accessible and has gone through the same experience, even
when counsel and sympathy are not far to seek, still men of the younger
generation being naturally prone to consider their case one of especial
hardship, prefer to nurse their own bitterness; and after a few years of
sneering at the possibility of American scholarship, they go the way of all
the rest, edit some over-edited school classic, translate some convenient
manual, get up a text-book of some sort, and in the lapse of time look
with half-pitying, half-envious eyes on the lads who come back from their
studies abroad conscious, as their elders were once, of a special divinity
within them. And this is the history of many of our best men—not all
their history, for it were not only foolish but criminal to measure a professor's efficiency simply by his written work. There is often a sublime self-
denial in the resolute concentration of a teacher on the business of a classroom; and the noiseless scholarship that leavens generation after
generation of pupils is of more value to the world of letters than folios of
pretentious erudition.

It may not be surprising that this attitude conveyed itself to even
the best students. Henry C. Allen writes home to his father on Dec. 7,
1856, "Prof. Gildersleeve, our new Prof. of Greek does not succeed very
well. He is young and there is room for improvement. Though a man of
ability he cannot impart his knowledge well to his class."[18] Significantly,
he adds, "This system is *new* and I fear that I cannot get through on
Greek." The difference from Harrison's method must have been jar-
ring. Harrison, after his period of bright promise, had long been reduced to teaching the grammatical basis of the language in rote exercise, which he considered more important than the reading of
literature.[19] Gildersleeve, on the other hand, came with the ability to
open "windows on Hellas. . . . We saw a living Hellas with that busy,
curious race of adventurous spirits which in olden times revealed to the
world the very pinnacles of beauty and wisdom and laid for the world

the ultimate foundations of truth and science."[20] These are the memories of William M. Thornton, Dean of Engineering and sketch-biogra-
pher par excellence, who describes the negative response Gildersleeve
received from those not among the most studious: "Perhaps at the first
his spirited pupils were jealous of his innovations. Perhaps he was a little
'too transcendental,'"[21] but more likely, he was a good deal too de-
manding:

> The two things which students in other Southern colleges heard most
> about in connection with the classical teaching in the University of Vir-
> ginia were the Greek and Latin prose compositions and the severity of the
> examinations. [Most universities stressed only a reading knowledge.] Dr.
> Gildersleeve's pupils prided themselves on the severity of his discipline,
> because they recognized in him a master who himself set an example of
> hard work; and they doubtless came to recognize the tasks expected of
> them as something of a personal compliment, as implying confidence in
> their ability. Then there was his wit to enliven the drudgery that is insepa-
> rable from some phases of hard work.[22]

Indeed, the early Gildersleeve could be downright (and uncharac-
teristically) haughty. An early student, W. J. N. Robinson, writes his
old teacher, Samuel Schooler:[23]

> Mynher [sic] Gildersleeve is now something more popular, and has
> thrown aside that boorish and supercilious manner which distinguished
> him so peculiarly before, acquired no doubt in the foreign method of the
> study of Greek which you described too truthfully in your last. And it is
> not without reason that he has done so. Some four weeks ago he treated a
> student rather cavalierly in open lecture, and much to his astonishment
> no doubt, he rec'd a little kind advice as to his conduct and a warning
> that it must not be repeated—The matter came up before the Faculty
> and Dame Rumor says that they rebuked Mr. G., told him his manner
> was peculiarly unfortunate, so much so as to have given offence to the
> ladies of the neighborhood and he must try to soften down some, at least
> touch his hat to a passing student—Now, I cannot vouch for the exact
> truth of *all* this, but certain it is, the affair has dropped, as it started as far
> as the student is concerned—

Remember that this is Gildersleeve at the age of 25. Even after the
sobering effects of the war, we find A. D. Savage, an early admiring
student of Gildersleeve, who went on to take degrees from Leipzig and
be one of the first Greek fellows at Johns Hopkins, writing to his father
in 1866, "Prof. Gildersleeve teaches so finely. . . . He and Dr. Maupin
are the only members of the faculty not generally liked as men. All the

others are very popular from their kind demeanor, treating the students as their equals."[24]

And Gildersleeve clearly walked into a professional conflict with Harrison. A later account in the University Archives cites one cause:[25]

> Harrison did not believe that the written accents handed down in the Greek manuscripts represented the real pronunciation of the ancients and so he accented Greek after the analogy of the Latin. The consequence was that when Dr. Gildersleeve introduced the Greek accents into the University of Virginia and thereby into the South, a serious obstacle confronted him. To give an account of the ensuing conflict would take up much space. Here at the University the conflict was promptly removed by the very personality of Dr. Gildersleeve with his extraordinary learning and brilliancy, but the conflict continued elsewhere between the teachers who used and the teachers who ignored the written accounts.

In any case, the "conflict" was also promptly removed by the resignation of Harrison in 1859. He left the University, tired and eclipsed by the brilliance of his younger colleague, to found a classical school for boys. While nursing an ailing son in 1862, Harrison contracted typhus and died on April 7 of that year.

Harrison was replaced by Lewis Minor Coleman, who held the Chair of Latin for only two years until he enlisted in the artillery of the Army of Northern Virginia and was killed at Fredericksburg, the only faculty member of the University to die in the war. In fact, Coleman and Gildersleeve were the only ones wounded.

This brings us to the war and its impact on the University. In 1860–1861 there were 604 students in residence; in the fall of 1861 only 66 matriculated and in 1862 only 46. Approximately half the professors entered some sort of war service, although it was felt that the University should stay open to train those who were wounded or too young to fight and also to help the war effort technologically (an abortive nitrate manufacturing processing lab was set up). The Chairs were doubled up by the remaining professors, and so Gildersleeve became Professor of Greek and Latin. His three (younger) brothers had all enlisted early in the war as privates: Benjamin in the First Virginia Cavalry; Gilbert, who rose to Captain of Cavalry under J. E. B. Stuart; and John, who, although a medical man, enlisted as a private also, but became assistant surgeon. Even their father, Rev. Benjamin Gildersleeve, at the age of 70, joined the Home Guard of Richmond.[26] All survived the war.

Despite his teaching duties, Basil joined in the summer, as an aide-de-camp to Col. Gilham in General Lee's Command in 1861, as a private in the First Virginia Cavalry with Benjamin in 1863, and as an aide (Captain) on General Gordon's staff in the Shenandoah Valley Campaign of 1864 under Jubal Early.[27] He thus, as he put it, earned "the right to teach Southern youths for nine months . . . by sharing the fortunes of their fathers and brothers at the front for three." He was proud "to have belonged in deed and truth to a heroic generation and to have shared in a measure its perils and privations."[28]

Both publicly and privately he called his war record "desultory."[29] However that may be, the skirmish at Weyer's Cave on September 25, 1864, brought the perils of war directly to Gildersleeve and identified him for years to come as a symbol of broken Southern nobility. While carrying orders to the front, he had his "thigh bone broken by a Spencer bullet,"[30] and his leg was nearly amputated. "I lost my pocket Homer, I lost my pistol, I lost one of my horses, and finally I came very near losing my life by a wound which kept me five months on my back."[31] Certainly he had joined because of the general enthusiasm and fraternal example, but also he undoubtedly heard the call of Goethe, whom he admired all his life.[32] In 1916, in one of the Brief Mentions, he discusses the passage in *Kampagne in Frankreich* that describes Goethe's desire to smell the actual gunsmoke in order to understand what *Kannonfever* was all about.[33]

And so he enlisted. The idea of involvement, of active participation, the acquisition of first-hand experience so central to Goethe may certainly have helped pitch Gildersleeve and many of the intellectuals of his generation into the fray. Certainly he may have needed a pocket Goethe less than a pocket Homer, for he appears to have nearly everything the German master wrote committed to memory. Gildersleeve describes a ride with a fellow officer accompanying Gordon to the front.[34]

> A man of winning appearance, sweet temper, and attractive manners, . . . I have never learned to love a man so much in so brief an acquaintance. . . . We rode together towards the front, and as we rode our talk fell on Goethe and on Faust, and of all the passages the soldier's song came to my lips, . . .
>     Kün ist das Mühen
>     Herrlich der Lohn.
> We reached the front. . . . Brief orders were given to the officer in command. My comrade was left to carry them out. The rest of us withdrew. Scarcely had we ridden a hundred yards toward camp when a shout was heard, and, turning round, we saw one of the men running after us. "The captain had been killed." The bullet had passed through his official papers and found his heart.

This, for Gildersleeve, was the worst kind of loss the war brought: the fine and educated youth which the South could never recover.

A memoir by Walter A. Montgomery, Professor of Latin at the University of Virginia from 1929 to 1942 and a student of Gildersleeve at Johns Hopkins, tells of Gildersleeve's five-month convalescence from his wounds: He slipped into despair and saw nothing ahead for an unreconstructed rebel but a Yankee-imposed exile.[35] He decided that he would join Maximilian's band of exiles, and he ardently threw himself into the study of Spanish. But Gildersleeve recovered his strength and spirits, keeping for life the limp that made him ever after associate himself with the "lame Spartan schoolmaster Tyrtaeus."

And happily Gildersleeve did not go off to Mexico; he threw himself with greater fervor and energy into the task of revising the American classical curriculum and improving its method of instruction. This, I think, is equally valuable to the task he set himself at Johns Hopkins University, to put American scholarship firmly upon the world stage and have its worth recognized internationally. To accomplish his goals, he first hired a Latinist, Thomas R. Price, to free his time; he began an intermediate level of Greek, raising the levels to three, and finally, he began to publish in his field. We might note here that in his first ten years at the University, he had published nothing on the subjects of his training, and it seems unlikely that in today's academic marketplace he would have received tenure or found it easier to secure employment than he had in 1853.

Within the next ten years he published the first and revised editions of his *Latin Grammar* (1867, 1872, 1894), *Latin Exercise-Book* (1871, 1873), *Latin Reader, Latin Primer* (both 1875), his edition of Persius (1875), and nine major articles (most collected in *Essays and Studies*) on all subjects for the *Southern Magazine* and the *Southern Review*. In addition to providing the texts for use in the classroom, he did his best to help supply teachers, principally by increasing the activity of his graduate program, one of the first of its kind in the nation.[36]

It should also be noted he fell in love with Elizabeth Fisher Colston, a beautiful blonde of a fine old Richmond family, as she nursed him recovering from his wounds at "Hillandale," the Colston estate in nearby Albemarle County, Virginia, where, on September 18, 1866, they were married. His devotion to her was singular, and they made their home at Pavilion I on the West Lawn a happy and contented one. They had four children, two of whom, Basil Seymour and Benjamin F., died in infancy, while Raleigh Colston grew up to become an architect in New York and Emma Louise married the son of the Harvard Latinist and former Göttingen schoolmate of Gildersleeve, George M. Lane. There was a painting of Mrs. Gildersleeve in the front hall of the Pavilion house which was a very poor likeness that did little credit to her beauty. Gildersleeve would often tell bewildered freshmen or confused visitors who could not make out the similarity that the woman in the painting was "the first Mrs. Gildersleeve." They must have made a wonderful sight walking up the lawn: he, tall and burly with a long thick black beard and dusky complexion to offset her fair features and dainty poise.[37]

To conclude: We might try to imagine what would have been the course of American classics if, by some chronological rearrangement, Gildersleeve had been able to go immediately from his German training to Johns Hopkins. Or more precisely, what did the University of Virginia do for him, and what did he do for the University of Virginia?

Looking back, he once said, "At the University of Virginia I learned what scholarship and toil meant in terms of growth and inner rewards."[38] He was forced to prepare nearly 70 lectures a semester with scant library facilities; he was forced to do his own primary reading, to do his own work without secondary literature or scholarly support; he was forced to cover all of Greek literature, language (at three levels), and Greek history each term, and for six years he had to do the same with Latin. He was forced into humane and friendly contact with students; he was forced to defend his beliefs in war; he compromised his time to the responsibilities, joys, and tragedies of family life. In truth, the University of Virginia cradled and nourished him as he matured from a precocious young man of 24 to the leading classicist of his united nation.

What he did for the University was to pass some 1800 students through arguably the most rigorous classics program in the South and continue the outstanding tradition begun by George Long and Mr. Jefferson. Without the demands made on his teaching at the undergraduate level, American classicists might not have profited from his vigorous defenses of the classics curriculum, nor been given his texts and grammars, so suited to our classrooms, nor had seven generations of eager classics teachers who thought not only of the library but also of the lecture hall.

His love of the University never left him. One of his students recalls that while at Hopkins, Gildersleeve was never once a minute late to class, much less absent. One day, however, he appeared in the doorway of his classroom, sans his academic impedimenta, and announced, "Gentlemen, I have just seen in the paper the calamity that has come to the institution where I taught for 20 years; there will be no lecture to-day."[39] This was October 1895, and the calamity was the burning of the Rotunda. The first letter and check received by then Dean Thornton for reconstruction was from Gildersleeve.

# NOTES

[1]I shall pass over, without repeating, the most famous story relating to BLG and the University. His remarks about finding eternal rest in Charlottesville may be found most recently in the *Johns Hopkins Magazine* (July 1974) 24 and *Virginia Cavalcade* 25 (Winter 1976) 116 and in this volume, Kennedy, p. 44.

[2]See "Formative Influences," *The Forum* 10 (1890-1891) 614; "Professorial Types," *The Hopkinsian* 1 (1893) 11-18; "A Novice of 1850," *Johns Hopkins Alumni Magazine* I,1 (Nov. 1912-June 1913) 3-9.

[3]"The College in the Forties," *Princeton Alumni Weekly* 16 (Jan. 26, 1916) 375.

[4]John Reuben Thompson (1823-1873) edited the *SLM* from 1847 until ill health forced him to resign in 1860. He spent a portion of the war in England, writing for the *Index* and *Blackwood's* and returned to become literary editor of the New York *Evening Post* until his death.

[5]"Formative Influences," 615-16.

[6]William M. Thornton, "Gildersleeve the Teacher," *Virginia Alumni Bulletin* 3rd ser. 17 (April 1924) 119. See also "The College in the Forties" (note 3 above) 376.

[7]Socrates Maupin (1809-1871) took an M.D. from the University in 1832, and after some years of teaching founded his own school in Richmond, for which he hired Gildersleeve for the school year between his graduation from Princeton and his departure for Germany (1849-1850).

[8]Thornton, ibid.

[9]On Long, see J. E. Sandys, *A History of Classical Scholarship* III (Cambridge 1908) 430.

[10]On Niebuhr, see Sandys, 77-82.

[11]H. B. Adams, *Thomas Jefferson and the University of Virginia* (Washington 1888), cited by Thornton (note 6 above) 121.

[12]Adams, ibid.

[13]G. Harrison, *An Exposition of Some of the Laws of the Latin Grammar* (New York 1852) [reprinted seven times between 1852 and 1868]. "It is sufficient to say that Long kept Dr. Harrison posted on all the latest German discoveries in philology and that the students of the University of Virginia were familiar with the labors of Bopp before that great man was fully recognized in Germany itself." W. P. Trent, *English Culture in Virginia*, Johns Hopkins University Studies in History and Political Science, Seventh Series, 5-6 (Baltimore 1889) 125; see also 89-94.

[14]P. A. Bruce, *History of the University of Virginia 1819-1919*, III (New York 1921) 34-35. Most of my information about the University, both general and statistical, comes from Bruce.

[15]John A. Broadus, *Sermons and Addresses* (Baltimore 1886), cited by Thornton (note 6 above) 122.

[16]Bruce, ibid. See also David M. R. Culbreth, M.D., *The University of Virginia: Memories of Her Student-Life and Professors* (New York 1908) 253: "There is something sublime in the spectacle of an unpretending, quiet, but deeply earnest and conscientious man, with the classical education of a great commonwealth or of the whole States, resting upon him, and slowly lifting up himself and his burden towards what they are capable of reaching. It was thus that Gessner Harrison toiled and suffered in this University for thirty-one years."

[17]"University Work in America and Classical Philology," *Princeton Review* 55 (May 1879) 515-17.

[18]H. C. Allen to John Allen (UVa accession no. 9780).

[19]Bruce (note 14 above) 36-37.

[20]Thornton (note 6 above) 129, also 127: "We were taught to see the skies of Hellas in the azure of our own Virginia heavens. . . . We were made to see in Manassas and Chancellorsville and Gettysburg and Appomattox an undying heroism akin to that of the Greeks 'who were first to face the danger at Marathon; who stood in the ranks at Plataea; who manned the decks of Salamis and Artemesium; who did all that brave men may do whose fate is that which God assigned.'" For an insight into the daily workings of an early Gildersleeve class, a student notebook of Micajah Woods remains from Gildersleeve's course on Tacitus *Annals*, Book III and G. K. Birchett, Jr.'s from a class in composition. Both are at the University.

[21]Thornton (note 6 above) 123. On 122-23, he quotes a letter of R. L. Harrison, the youngest son of Gessner and a student of Gildersleeve, that "some criticized his method as too transcendental for American students."

[22]C. F. Smith, "Dr. Gildersleeve Early Revealed Qualities that Made Him Great," Charleston (SC) *News and Courier*, Jan. 13, 1924, p. 20.

[23]Dated Feb. 11, 1857. Letter in William R. Perkins Library, Duke University.

[24]November 11, 1866 (UVa accession no. 10019).

[25]A six-page biographical sketch, author unknown (UVa accession no. 9315).

[26]"Formative Influences," 608.

[27]J. B. Gordon, *Reminiscences of the Civil War* (New York 1905) 422.

[28]"Creed of the Old South," 75.

[29]"A Southerner in the Peloponnesian War," 334: "my short and desultory service in the field"; and letter to Thornton of Feb. 15, 1908 (UVa accession no. 2077-B): "a very desultory affair."

[30]*AJP* 22 (1901) 468 (=*Gildersleeve 6*, 75).

[31]"Formative Influences," 616.

[32]John T. Krumpelmann, *Southern Scholars in Goethe's Germany* (Chapel Hill 1965) 104-33.

[33]"Goethe tells us that he rode into the zone of the great guns in order to find out for himself what is meant by 'cannon fever,' and so Gildersleeve 'tried to analyze [his] own feelings under similar circumstances.'" "Brief Mention," *AJP* 37 (1916) 372-73.

[34]"Creed of the Old South," 76-77. The lines are *Faust* 899-900.

[35]Dr. Walter A. Montgomery, "My Recollections of Basil L. Gildersleeve," two records, side 3 (UVa accession no. 8734).

[36]See Mary Bynum Pierson, *Graduate Work in the South* (Chapel Hill 1947) 34-35, 57-59; Richard J. Storr, *The Beginnings of Graduate Education in America* (Chicago 1953) 157, n. 45.

[37]For a further physical description of Gildersleeve, see Culbreth (note 16 above) 397-98.

[38]Montgomery (note 35 above) side 2. See also Gildersleeve's impromptu farewell remarks to the faculty and students as quoted by Culbreth (note 16 above) 401: "I had not thought of saying farewell to you till I should bid the world good-night. Here to me love, labor and sorrow have found their keenest expression. . . .I may have spoken many ill-advised words since coming here, but have spoken naught in malice. I think I may say without fear of contradiction that I have striven faithfully to do my best; I hope some of my old pupils are not altogether ashamed of their preceptor; for them, at least, my heart swells with pride, and if I have turned out in the twenty years of my professional career only the one noble scholar who is to succeed me, I shall not think my life a failure. To the University I shall give my allegiance, her fame is mine, and her lofty standard of morals, her unswerving adherence to truth and purity, and all high and noble learning shall be my standard forever."

[39]Montgomery (note 35 above) side 3. See also W. M. Thornton, "Basil Lanneau Gildersleeve at the University of Virginia," *Johns Hopkins Alumni Magazine* 13, 2 (January 1925) 125.

# THE FOUNDATION OF JOHNS HOPKINS AND THE FIRST FACULTY

Herbert W. Benario

We do not know when the idea for a university that was to bear his name came to the mind of the Baltimore merchant Johns Hopkins. The first tangible date is 1867, when he requested twelve fellow citizens to incorporate themselves as "The Johns Hopkins University." Perhaps more meaningful a date is 1870, when he signed his will, which spoke, in large terms if briefly, of the institution he envisaged.[1] It may be that 1874 is an even truer date, for it was in that year that, after Mr. Hopkins' death, the probating of his will made his bequest official. But the year that was ultimately chosen as the beginning of the University is 1876, on February 22 to be precise, the day on which Daniel Coit Gilman was inaugurated as the first president.[2]

It was Gilman's vision, after a brief and unhappy tenure at the University of California, to develop a university based on the model of the distinguished foundations of Germany, concerned in the first instance with the promotion of scholarship at the highest level and in the second with advanced instruction only. He desired an institution unlike any then in existence in the United States, which would rise far above collegiate instruction. This would require a faculty of the first rank, men of original genius and talent who were presently compelled "to pass most of their time teaching the rudiments to boys, or preparing school-books."[3]

The Hopkins trustees, faced with such an enthusiastic and novel proposal when they first interviewed Gilman, were not struck dumb. They were much taken by this philosopher of education who came highly recommended by Charles W. Eliot of Harvard, Andrew D. White of Cornell, and James B. Angell of Michigan, who, consulted individually, each recommended Gilman as the man to lead the new foundation. They responded by doing what all administrators and faculties invariably wish all boards would do: they elected him and gave him full support in his difficult task. No part of that task was of greater significance than the selection of a faculty.

Since the will of Johns Hopkins had established a medical school as well as a university, President Gilman was naturally concerned with the appointment of men in the sciences. He recognized the possibility and need for research on the cutting edge of knowledge, to use an expression so popular in our day, and sought out men both at the heights and the beginnings of their careers in the laboratory sciences and in mathematics.[4] With mathematics, however, stood philology as one of the disciplines in which Germany had demonstrated particular eminence. Since the days of Edward Everett more than half a century earlier, young Americans had been compelled to travel to Germany if they desired advanced work in the languages of antiquity. George Ticknor,[5] his contemporary, said in 1816, "We are mortified and exasperated because we have no learned men, and yet make it *physically* impossible for our scholars to become such, and that to escape from this reproach we appoint a multitude of professors, but give them a library from which hardly one and *not* one of them can qualify himself to execute the duties of his office."[6]

Greek dominated Latin in the Germany of the nineteenth century;[7] the legacy of Friedrich August Wolf continued without significant challenge, even with the Roman historical work of Niebuhr and Mommsen and the textual achievements of Lachmann. The more gentlemanly approach in Great Britain, or less scholarly, as many would charge, recognized the same relationship between the languages, where Oxford had had a Regius Professor of Greek since the days of Henry VIII but a Professor of Latin only since the middle of the century.[8] Greek was paramount. Whom would Gilman seek? His first choice, it may surprise some to learn, was William Watson Goodwin of Harvard.

Goodwin had been born in May 1831, had gone to Germany to study in 1853, consecutively at Göttingen, Bonn, and Berlin, and had been awarded the doctorate from Göttingen in 1855. The following year he was appointed tutor at Harvard and in 1860 was elevated to the Eliot chair of Greek in succession to Cornelius C. Felton. That year saw the publication of the *Syntax of the Moods and Tenses of the Greek Verb*, a work which still endures in honor and importance and which was to prove the chief achievement of his long and distinguished career. It is perhaps most significant in the present context because of the great contrast between it and the works of his predecessor in the Eliot chair, who is best remembered for publications that are rather *haute vulgarisation* and for elementary textbooks.[9] The impact of German philological training was now clearly evidenced.

Goodwin expressed interest in the professorship that Gilman held before him, and even inquired about life in Baltimore. But at the end, although the attractions of the new position were great, he decided to stay in Cambridge, until his retirement in 1901.[10]

Stymied in his raiding expedition to the north, Gilman looked to the south, to Mr. Jefferson's university, where the Professor of Greek since 1856 had been Basil L. Gildersleeve. Born only a half year after Goodwin, he had nonetheless anticipated the latter in study abroad. After graduating from Princeton in 1849, he went to Berlin and Bonn before receiving his Ph.D. from Göttingen in 1853. His return home was not greeted by a teaching post, and he despaired of an academic career until the call from Virginia came. There his duties were largely concerned with instruction at what would properly be called elementary levels, much concerned particularly with grammar and syntax, and during the grim years of civil strife he also fulfilled the duties of the professorship of Latin, from 1861 to 1866. From these years came his *Latin Grammar* (1867) as well as his series of Latin textbooks.

Gilman invited Gildersleeve to a meeting in Washington on December 8, 1875. It was clearly a satisfactory experience for both, for three days later Gildersleeve accepted the offer of the chair of Greek. He wrote Gilman on the latter occasion, "To such confidence as you have reposed in me, my whole nature responds with all its earnestness and I shall enter upon my new duties with heightened interest because my success will be in a measure yours."[11] The philosophies of the two men were unquestionably compatible, and Gildersleeve must have relished the prospect of advanced instruction. He soon wrote to the President, "As I understand my new work, my lowest level is to be the upper tier of my present senior class in which I am doing some real University work. It will take two or three years of earnest effort to get our material up to that point. After that time I should not despair of fair success in the University part of our scheme."[12]

The formal appointment of Gildersleeve came on January 17, 1876. This made him in fact the first professor of the new University,[13] although he was not the first with whom negotiations had been begun. Appointments in mathematics, physics, chemistry, and biology soon followed. Designation of a professor of Latin was still a desideratum, but Gilman was disappointed in his first attempts to win a man of eminence. Soon the name of Charles d'Urban Morris was brought to his attention. Trained at Lincoln College, Oxford, and a former fellow of Oriel, he was then professor at the University of the City of New York (now NYU). He was recommended as "among the half dozen best Classical Scholars in England or America, and an admirable tutor of College students. He has through a series of unfortunate accidents been wasted on boys."[14] He was originally appointed at Hopkins as Associate Professor of Greek and Latin, but the title was soon changed to Colle-

giate Professor. Morris' responsibilities were with the lower levels of instruction in both languages, and finally it was he who represented Latin
in the classical field. The first Professor of Latin was not designated for
a decade, until the appointment in 1886 of Minton Warren, who had
been director of the Latin Seminary since 1879.

Morris was a great success, complementing Gildersleeve admira-
bly.[15] Gilbert Highet, in his well-known book, *The Art of Teaching*,
tells of Abraham Flexner, who years later became famous for his influential report on medical education in the United States; he was told by
Morris

> that if he wanted to master Greek, he should get a compact little shelf of
> Greek books and read nothing but Greek for five years. "Read the daily
> papers to keep up with the world," he said, "but don't read books in any
> other language. Read Greek only." The ambitious young student took
> this hard advice, and . . . he gazed at the intricate subject until he really
> felt at home in it . . . he could pick up a book (an immortal book, a
> permanently valuable book) in Greek, and read it through with ease and
> pleasure. Such efforts are painful; but without effort there is no reward.[16]

President Gilman's vision and powers of selection and persuasion
were amply rewarded: "Johns Hopkins began at the top."[17] These are
the words of E. G. Sihler, who was one of the choice five who comprised
Gildersleeve's initial group of students and who went on to a long and
productive career at New York University. The beginning of the first
course of instruction was delayed until December 5, because
Gildersleeve gave a course of public lectures on Greek lyric poetry. The
subject of the *seminarium* was Thucydides, and soon thereafter
Gildersleeve began his lectures on historical Greek syntax, drawn from
material he had steadily gathered during the years in Charlottesville.
The master flourished in his first years at Hopkins; his edition of Justin
Martyr appeared in 1877, the first Ph.D. in Greek was awarded in 1878;
the *American Journal of Philology* was founded in 1880;[18] and the great
Pindar was published in 1885. In the interim he was president of the
American Philological Association in 1877–1878 and was offered the
directorship of the newly founded American School of Classical Studies
in Athens. He had found contentment with students worthy of his tal-
ents. As editor of the *Journal*, the only scholarly publication in the
United States devoted to philology in its broadest sense, he was now perhaps the most distinguished and influential classicist in the United
States.

Not that there were not some disturbing factors. The University was heavily skewed toward the sciences, nor had the appointment of a Professor of Latin of a stature approximating Gildersleeve's ensued. Classics at Hopkins in those first years was one-sided, but that side offered the best that was available. In 1891, Gildersleeve wrote, "The greater freedom of action, the larger appliances, the wider and richer life, the opportunities for travel and for personal intercourse have stimulated production and have made my last fourteen years my most fruitful years in the eyes of the scholarly world."[19]

The opportunity and the man were indeed well matched. Gilman gave Gildersleeve the chance to escape from the humdrum labors of elementary tuition and to allow his genius and imagination to soar. His career at Hopkins as an active professor spanned thirty-nine years. What he accomplished during that period is known, at least in outline, to everyone. In 1919 Paul Shorey, in his famous paper, "Fifty Years of Classical Studies in America," spoke of Germany's, England's, and America's preeminent scholars, Wilamowitz, Jebb, and Gildersleeve. Of the last he said,

> In sheer insight into the structure and genius of the Greek language he has no equal. . . . No English-speaking scholar can teach Greek without plagiarizing Gildersleeve's phrases and formulas . . . you can hardly pick up a number of Brief Mention, even among those which an unfriendly critic might deem the most discursive, frivolous, and repetitious, without learning something about Greek or the history of literature or linguistic analysis and literary criticism, that is worth knowing and that you did not know, without receiving some suggestion that will prove of helpful application in your own reading and study.[20]

Had it been possible, Gilman would have looked from the Elysian Fields at the institution he shaped and would have smiled. On the philological side, he had certainly chosen well when gathering his first faculty.

# NOTES

[1]One of the few definite instructions to the Trustees made in the will is that a "judicious" number of scholarships be given to students from Maryland, Virginia, and North Carolina. *Johns Hopkins University: Charter, Extracts of Will, Officers, and By-Laws* (Baltimore 1874); Hugh Hawkins, *Pioneer: A History of the Johns Hopkins University, 1874–1889* (Ithaca, NY 1960) 3–4.

[2]The fullest reports are in John C. French, *A History of the University Founded by Johns Hopkins* (Baltimore 1946) and Hawkins.

[3]From Gilman's account of his first encounter with the Trustees in *The Nation*,

Jan. 28, 1875, quoted in Fabian Franklin, *The Life of Daniel Coit Gilman* (New York 1910) 188.

[4]Of the first four appointments, Gildersleeve was the only humanist. James J. Sylvester in mathematics, Henry Rowland in Physics, and Ira Remsen in Chemistry completed the "Hopkins Four"; see K. A. Jacob, "The Hopkins Four," *Johns Hopkins Magazine* (July 1974) 17-26.

[5]For sketches of the careers of both Everett and Ticknor, see Orie William Long, *Literary Pioneers. Early American Explorers of European Culture* (Cambridge, MA 1935), and, for Everett, Meyer Reinhold, "A 'New Morning': Edward Everett's Contributions to Classical Learning," *CO* 59 (1981-1982) 37-41(= *Classica Americana* [Detroit 1984] 204-13); and in this volume, Newmyer, p. 29, n. 9.

[6]Long (note 5 above) 13.

[7]See E. M. Butler, *The Tyranny of Greece over Germany* (New York 1935).

[8]John Conington was appointed in 1856.

[9]Felton (1807-1862) held the Eliot chair from 1834 to 1860, when he was made President of Harvard. He is best known for his lectures given at the Lowell Institute in Boston (1852-1859), *Greece: Ancient and Modern* 2 vols. (Boston 1867), and two textbooks, *Selections from the Greek Historians* (Cambridge, MA 1852) and *A Greek Reader for the Use of Schools* (Hartford, CT 1840). Both of the latter were reprinted for thirty years after their publication.

[10]Hawkins (note 1 above) 49-50. On Goodwin, see Charles Burton Gulick, *DAB* VII, 411-13, and in this volume, Fowler, p. 93, n. 4.

[11]Gildersleeve to Gilman, Dec. 11, 1875, cited by Hawkins (note 1 above) 51. Gilman had visited Charlottesville in the spring of 1875 (see Hawkins, 31) and clearly had his eye on Gildersleeve: "I may be forgiven for bringing forth my treasured remembrance of the hour when we first met in my old academic home, and when, all unsuspected by me, he was taking my measure for the office I was destined to fill." ("Address," *Daniel Coit Gilman: First President of the Johns Hopkins University 1876–1901* [Baltimore 1908] 34.)

[12]Gildersleeve to Gilman, Dec. 30, 1875, cited by Hawkins, ibid.

[13]Hawkins, ibid.

[14]Hawkins (note 1 above) 52.

[15]Idem.

[16]G. Highet, *The Art of Teaching* (New York 1950) 244.

[17]Ernest G. Sihler, *From Maumee to Thames and Tiber* (New York 1930) 96. Sihler was the first Ph.D. in Greek from Johns Hopkins and, of the original five Fellows in Greek—Charles R. Lanman, Walter Hines Page, Arthur D. Savage, Sihler, and John H. Wheeler—only Sihler completed the degree. Lanman already had a Ph.D. from Yale (1873), and Wheeler went on to take his doctorate from Bonn in 1879.

[18]French (note 2 above) 54-55; Hawkins (note 1 above) 108.

[19]"Formative Influences," *The Forum* 10 (Feb. 1891) 617.

[20]*TAPA* 50 (1919) 60.

# GILDERSLEEVE ON THE STUDY OF THE CLASSICS

Stephen Newmyer

A few months after the death of Basil Gildersleeve in January 1924, his former student and colleague as Professor of Greek at the Johns Hopkins University, Charles William Emil Miller, published an obituary in the *American Journal of Philology* in which he wrote of his honored friend:

> It was inevitable that a man of such keenness of intellect, versatility of genius, wealth of knowledge, catholicity of taste, mobility of tempera-ment and breadth of human experience should have been an inspiring teacher. The years spent as a student under Professor Gildersleeve were years of intellectual intoxication. Enthusiasm never waned. Inspiration was an incentive to study. The spur of reprimand and correction was not needed. And how deep was the affection and the reverence for the teacher! . . . He was everywhere called master by those who themselves were masters, and in the American classical pantheon he sat enthroned as Zeus.[1]

What Miller primarily singles out for praise in this passage, his subject's skill as a teacher, is that most fragile part of a scholar's legacy, that part sometimes slighted by a posterity which often estimates a scholar solely on the basis of his weightier publications. Yet, if we may judge by the frequency and vehemence with which Gildersleeve spoke on the subject, the pedagogical aspect of classical study interested him quite as deeply as did the purely philological. For Gildersleeve, the question of excellence in teaching formed a central element in a wider concern for the betterment of the status of classical study in America and for the production of highly trained teacher-scholars to effect that improvement.

Gildersleeve addressed the question of the study of the classics from the beginning of his professional career, in his youthful essay enti-tled "Necessity of the Classics,"[2] to his presidential address before the American Philological Association in 1909 entitled "The Range and Character of the Philological Activity of America"[3] and his book *Hellas and Hesperia*,[4] which appeared that same year. Although more than half a century separates his earliest and latest pronouncements on the subject, Gildersleeve's message and concerns are remarkably uniform throughout his career. He devoted considerable energy, especially in the earlier stages of his career, to polemical defenses of classical study against some of those forces which he felt most threatened the progress of the discipline in this country—the political-minded scientism of America, the nation's general anti-intellectual tenor, and the large number of influential voices who attacked the discipline as esoteric and useless. As Gildersleeve's career advanced, however, he focused his attention more directly upon an issue of fundamental interest to him: how was America to find its niche in the discipline, and how could American classical studies earn a place of honor beside the philology of other nations? As late as 1878, in his presidential address before the American Philological Association in Saratoga Springs, New York,[5] Gildersleeve almost despaired of America's ever finding a place of respect in classical studies, but by 1909, when he again addressed the Association as President, he could say with pride that what he had hoped for the profession in America had been attained.[6]

The source of Gildersleeve's early doubts was his first-hand acquaintance with German philology during his study years in Europe. For him, as for earlier generations of youthful Americans who had made the pilgrimage to the home of *Altertumswissenschaft*, Germany was both the inspiration and the despair of hopeful American philologists. In later years, he never tired of recalling his first impressions of his magisterial professors at Berlin, Göttingen, and Bonn, and he gratefully acknowledged his debt to his German training. In his autobiographical sketch, "Formative Influences," Gildersleeve wrote, "To Germany and the Germans I am indebted for everything professionally, in the way of apparatus and of method, and for much, very much, in the way of inspiration."[7]

In his essay "Necessity of the Classics," published in 1854, shortly after his return to the United States, Gildersleeve surveyed "the condition of classical study in our country,"[8] and he gave voice to some of the doubts that he felt for America's future in classical studies. Writing only two generations after America's first foreign-trained classicists returned from Germany, he shared the enthusiasm of such earlier innocents abroad as Edward Everett and Cornelius Felton for introducing German-style philology into American schools,[9] but he was not blind to the shortcomings of America's efforts heretofore in this direction. "The Germans are now dominant in the science of classical philology," he wrote, "and we must harmonize with them or make a senseless discord.

. . . We have shown a willingness to receive, and a readiness to apply, the teachings of Germany, which contrasts favourably with the obstinacy of the English. Unfortunately, however, this receptivity has been, thus far, confined to a wholesale appropriation of the results, instead of an adoption and application of the method."[10]

The conditions that produced the sort of imitative hackwork in the 1830s and '40s which he censures here had not greatly improved when Gildersleeve inaugurated his own career. Every American who returned from Germany lamented the inadequacy of American libraries, the lack of thoroughly trained teachers, and the imperfect knowledge of the classical languages that remained the hallmarks of classical study in America in the 1850s and '60s. Basil Gildersleeve fell heir to what Meyer Reinhold has aptly called the "Silver Age of Classical Study in America,"[11] the decades from 1790 to 1830, which questioned the pertinence of classical study to the life of the nation and pointed with disgust to the superficiality of classical training in the United States. Reinhold remarks on this Silver Age, "Before American classical studies could attain to its 'Heroic Age' a generation later, it needed the courage and learning of a Basil Gildersleeve, who could say, even if retrospectively, of the state of classical learning in his student days in the mid-nineteenth century '. . . my American teachers did not understand their business.'"[12]

No less discouraging to Gildersleeve in the earlier years of his professional career was the chorus of influential voices, some within academe, who questioned the value of the classics in the college curriculum. One such enemy of the classics was a Dr. Bigelow, a professor at Harvard and President of the American Academy of Arts and Sciences, who was the object of Gildersleeve's pointed scorn in his article "Limits of Culture."[13] He defended the profession here with some of the same arguments marshalled today by beleaguered classicists, arguing that a classical education exerted a humanizing influence, developed a force of continuity in historical perspective, made our own literature live through allusion, and inculcated syntactic exactness in its students. In 1878, in "Classics and Colleges,"[14] he again defended the discipline, now against Mark Pattison, who had remarked in the previous year in the *Fortnightly Review* that extensive study of Greek and Latin had exerted little positive effect on the graceless style of the Germans who studied the classics. That, Gildersleeve countered, was hardly the fault of the classics, but rather of the less than genius types who studied them. The real shortcomings of the profession, as Gildersleeve saw them, were

due not to the inferiority of the subject matter but to "the lack of independent research, the wholesale conveyance of foreign work, the limited
range of study, the mechanical multiplication of text-books, the want of
honest, manly criticism."[15]

The foundation of the American Philological Association in 1869
and Gildersleeve's appointment in 1876 as Professor of Greek at the
newly founded Johns Hopkins University were encouraging signs that
America's classicists had come to recognize the sad state of their profession and were mobilizing to improve the situation, but Gildersleeve was
fully aware that the profession had thereby only begun the process of
revitalization. In 1878, as President for the first time of the fledgling
Association, he set forth to his colleagues the program he envisioned for
the rebirth of the profession.

His address "University Work in America and Classical Philology," published in 1879, has been called by George Kennedy "the Charter of American classical scholarship."[16] Prominent in that charter is
Gildersleeve's vision of the American professor of classics. "An able ex-
plorer may be an indifferent teacher," Gildersleeve observed, "a good
teacher may not have the spirit of initiative which leads to successful
investigation; but the two faculties, though not always in perfect bal-
ance, are seldom divorced, and a university professor should possess
both."[17] Unfortunately, the American classroom in Gildersleeve's day,
with its emphasis on rote memory and drill, was scarcely calculated to
afford the teacher stimulus to excellence or the scholar inspiration to
research, and Gildersleeve admitted that many a self-sacrificing investigator would in desperation abandon all thought of significant research
and devote his career to quiet teaching. Nor was such an individual to
be scorned. "The noiseless scholarship that leavens generation after
generation of pupils," Gildersleeve noted, "is of more value to the world
of letters than folios of pretentious erudition."[18]

If young scholars eager to discover new truths could not yet find all
the research materials they needed in the understocked libraries of
American colleges and universities, he hoped that they could at least
find inspiration and stimulation in the comradeship of fellow classicists.
To this end Gildersleeve recommended the creation of local and regional classical associations, of both a formal and an informal nature.
The APA was of course a helpful start, "but everybody knows," he observed, "that these companies of scholars [the APA and its "elder sister,"
the American Oriental Society] depend for their existence on the personal influence and reputation of a few distinguished men, and the

meetings are too infrequent, the attendance too meagre, and the elements too varying to encourage the hope that the redemption of philology for which we pray is to come from them."[19] Small, even informal gatherings could alleviate this situation and, in a setting where young and older scholars could interact, could help the young scholars to ready their work for publication under the careful guidance of their elder colleagues.

The chief stumbling block to America's progress in the profession appeared to Gildersleeve to lie in a certain diffidence on the part of Americans to exert themselves in a field so dominated by Europeans. In "University Work in America and Classical Philology," Gildersleeve poses the question that was fundamental to his program for resurrecting classics in this country: does America, after all, have anything to offer the profession? "Let us now look," he wrote in that essay, "at the sphere of research and ask, Is there any work for Americans to do in the department of classical philology—any work for which they are especially fitted either by natural bent or peculiar environment? Or, to put the question in its mildest form, Is there any work in which they are not at too great a disadvantage as compared with their European brethren?"[20] He answered with a firm *yes*. Americans, Gildersleeve felt, are particularly suited to take a leading position in the profession because of their natural receptivity and inquisitiveness, free from the pedantry of the Germans, the skepticism of the English, and the erratic manner of the French. But first America must assert its freedom from excessive dependence on foreign (and most especially German) influence. "In order to walk," he argued, "we must stand on our feet, and, so standing, discard the leading strings which so many like to feel, even if they do not lean on them."[21]

Gildersleeve never tired of stating that, so long as texts of the ancient authors were available to them, Americans could always claim a place of respect as painstaking interpreters of the languages, politics, and society of antiquity. He prophesied, "The way to better things is open, and if the younger generation of American university students will walk in it, if close acquaintance with the sources become the great characteristic of our philology, American books will receive higher approval from foreign critics than the half-pitying commendation with which they recognize the faithful use of the most recent German works on the subjects treated."[22] He suggested that Americans could earn an exalted place as interpreters of recently discovered inscriptions, and that the unique nature of America's history rendered our philologists particularly fit to interpret the ancient historical experience. American keenness of intellect and boldness of mind could render our scholars expert in syntactical and lexicographical studies, areas of classical philology which Gildersleeve felt remained in his day virtually untouched in English.

The program that Gildersleeve outlined in "University Work in America and Classical Philology" marks a clear movement away from the Teutonomania that distinguished his views on the profession immediately after his return from Germany. Gildersleeve's vision for the future of classical studies in this country was now founded on what, in the Brief Mention published in the *American Journal of Philology* in 1916, he would come to term "Americanism."[23] It involved an eclectic approach to classical studies that incorporated the best of the German, French, and English methods while avoiding their shortcomings. In an essay (later entitled "Americanism"), he wrote of this vision, "I . . . have over and over again urged as our American mission the blending of all the schools."[24] Americanism was, besides this, an attitude toward the study of the classics which had as its guiding principle a broad humanism that renounced the narrow specialization and dry pedantry that plagued German philology. The American classicist must keep ever before him the ennobling and inspiring values of the classics which entitle them to be the foundation of any college curriculum. "No one, teacher or scholar," he warned in "University Work in America and Classical Philology," "should so lose himself in grammatical and critical studies as to become insensible of the deep truth which is embodied in the old term, the 'humanities.'"[25]

Beginning in 1893, with the publication of his article "Professorial Types" in *The Hopkinsian*,[26] and culminating in his second presidential address before the APA in 1909, Gildersleeve took a series of backwards glances at the progress of the profession in the decades since he had formulated his charter in 1878, and he noted with satisfaction that his goals had been at least in part realized. In the abstract of that presidential address, which was titled "The Range and Character of the Philological Activity of America," Gildersleeve wrote of his early concerns, "How needless now the preachment of the Presidential Address of 1878, how ample the fulfilment of the prophecy. Then it was timely to plead for the establishment of local Philological Societies. Now they dot the land. . . . Every eye can mark the tide of life that has carried American work to European shores. . . ."[27] He could even reflect that the success of American scholarship in the eyes of the world could be attributed to those special talents which he had long ago marked out as the hope of American classical studies, namely "this quickness to appreciate, this eagerness to assimilate, this openmindedness, this 'clear vision and straight thought' that may be set down as specifically American, and as lending to all our work a truly national stamp."[28]

Much of the credit for the progress which America had made in classical philology in that half-century must, indeed, rest with Gildersleeve himself. By establishing the *American Journal of Philology*, he had assured that the researches of Americans could see the light of day, and in its early years the journal specialized in those very syntactical and lexicographical studies that Gildersleeve had particularly recommended to American scholars. The foundation of the Johns Hopkins University facilitated the production of the sort of teachers whom Gildersleeve considered essential to his program of revitalization. In "Professorial Types," he lauded the part played by Johns Hopkins in creating the "professionalism of the professorship."[29] No longer did classicists need to be trained as mathematicians who kept up their Greek in case a professorship in Greek fell vacant. "It is better that the professor should be a professional man," he wrote, "and should have received a training with special reference to his calling in life and, to this distinct recognition of the professorship as a career, we Hopkinsians think that our University has made a decided contribution, though, as individuals, we must always endeavor to widen our sympathies and strive to apprehend something of the great movement of the world outside of our special lines of work."[30] In his article "Oscillations and Nutations of Philological Studies,"[31] he examined the ups and downs of classical philology in America in the period 1850 to 1900 and noted that the enormous growth of knowledge concerning antiquity in that half-century rendered some degree of specialization a practical necessity, but he again urged that classicists not lose sight of the broader goals of their discipline. "I would reiterate the confession of my faith in the formulae of my youth, my belief in the wider conception of philological work, in the necessity of bringing all our special investigations into relation with the whole body of philological truth, the life of the world, the life of humanity."[32]

The responsibility for this weighty task lay upon the teacher whose training and knowledge were nothing if he could not inspire the pupils in his charge. Gildersleeve wrote in "Classical Studies in America" in 1896, "The teacher who does not rise from the particular to the universal, whose special line of research is not a line of fire as well as a line of light, who leaves his students as cold as he found them, does not live up to the measure of his prophetic office."[33] In his Page-Barbour Lectures at the University of Virginia, which appeared in 1909 as the volume *Hellas and Hesperia*, Gildersleeve, in the course of leisurely musings on many aspects of his discipline, touched repeatedly on the life's work of the teacher and concluded that, beyond all else, the teacher must spark in his pupils his love for his subject. "The lessons are lost," he wrote, "the love abides, and love is life."[34] That love, as is clear from Miller's obituary, Gildersleeve instilled in his pupils in abundant measure, and the discipline that Gildersleeve loved afforded him the broader vision of humanity and of the oneness of the ancient and modern experience which he hoped classical study would bring to all who devoted their lives to it. In *Hellas and Hesperia* he summed up his own career in the service of the classics, "Every manifestation of national life has its answering manifestation in every other. This is the bread of life and the water of life that have sustained me as they have sustained others through the aridities of a wilderness of study, and if that on which my eyes have gazed is not Plato's ocean of the beautiful, but a mirage, I thank God for that mirage."[35]

# NOTES

[1]C. W. E. Miller, "Basil Lanneau Gildersleeve," *AJP* 45 (1924) 100.

[2]"Necessity of the Classics," *Southern Quarterly Review* 26 (n.s. 10) (1854) 145–67, a review article of G. Bernhardy's *Grundriss der Griechischen Litteratur*, vol. I (Halle 1852).

[3]"The Range and Character of the Philological Activity of America," *TAPA* 40 (1909) xxxviii–xxxix. This is an abstract of Gildersleeve's address delivered before the APA on December 28, 1909.

[4]*Gildersleeve 4*.

[5]This address was published under the title "University Work in America and Classical Philology," *Princeton Review* 55 (1879) 511–36 (=*Gildersleeve 2*, 87–123).

[6]In "The Range and Character of the Philological Activity of America" (note 3 above) xxxxviii, for example, Gildersleeve asserts that in 1909 Americans can "sit in judgement on their European fellows and . . . make their verdict respected."

[7]"Formative Influences," *The Forum* 10 (1891) 615.

[8]"Necessity of the Classics" (note 2 above) 157.

[9]On the enthusiasm of Edward Everett and Cornelius Felton for German philology, see Meyer Reinhold, "A 'New Morning': Edward Everett's Contributions to Classical Learning," *CO* 59 (1981–1982) 37–41, and David S. Wiesen, "Cornelius Felton and the Flowering of the Classics in New England," *CO* 59 (1981–1982) 44–48.

[10]"Necessity of the Classics," 161–63.

[11]Meyer Reinhold, "The Silver Age of Classical Studies in America, 1790–1830," in *Ancient and Modern: Essays in Honor of Gerald F. Else* (Ann Arbor 1977) 181–213.

[12]Ibid., 212–13. The quotation from Gildersleeve is found in the Brief Mention at *AJP* 37 (1916) 495 (=*Gildersleeve 6*, 365, where it is entitled "English and German Scholarship").

[13]"Limits of Culture," *Southern Review* 2 (1867) 421–48 (=*Gildersleeve 2*, 3–40).

[14]"Classics and Colleges," *Princeton Review* 54 (1878) 67–95 (=*Gildersleeve 2*, 43–84).

[15]Ibid., 79 (=*Gildersleeve 2*, 61). The article in question is Pattison's "Books and Critics," *Fortnightly Review* 28 (n.s. 22) (Nov. 1877) 659–79, which was reprinted in this country in *Eclectic Magazine of Foreign Literature* n.s. 27 (1878) 93–106 and *Popular Science Monthly Supplement* VII–XII (1878) 159–71.

[16]See, in this volume, Kennedy, p. 44.

[17]"University Work in America and Classical Philology," 514 (=*Gildersleeve 2*, 91).

[18]Ibid., 517 (=*Gildersleeve 2*, 96).

[19]Ibid., 517–18 (=*Gildersleeve 2*, 96–97).

[20]Ibid., 519 (=*Gildersleeve 2*, 98–99).

[21]Ibid., 523 (=*Gildersleeve 2*, 104).

[22]Ibid., 522–23 (=*Gildersleeve 2*, 104).

[23]*AJP* 37 (1916) 113–15 (=*Gildersleeve 6*, 340–42, where it is entitled "Americanism").

[24]Ibid., 114.

[25]"University Work in America and Classical Philology," 536 (=*Gildersleeve 2*, 123). See also in this volume, Fowler p. 90.

[26]"Professorial Types," *The Hopkinsian* 1 (1893) 11–18.

[27]See note 3 above.

[28]Ibid., xxxix.

[29]"Professorial Types," 11.

[30]Ibid., 13.

[31]"Oscillations and Nutations of Philological Studies," *Johns Hopkins University Circulars* 20 (1901) 45–50.

[32]Ibid., 50.

[33]"Classical Studies in America," *Atlantic Monthly* 78 (1896) 731.

[34]*Gildersleeve 4*, 40.

[35]Ibid., 43.

# GILDERSLEEVE THE SYNTACTICIAN

John Vaio

The syntactically knowing Hellenist — reader too of that eminent monthly, *Gentlemen's Quarterly* — might make the following observation. Use of Kühner is comparable to frequenting that bastion of conservative men's wear, Brooks Brothers, with an eye to somber hues and lines.[1] Turn to Goodwin's *Moods*, and a walk across Manhattan's 44th Street to J. Press, a still traditional but somewhat livelier clothier, might add a little color and variety.[2] But what of that self-considerate aesthetician of fashion who regularly buys his first-class ticket to Milan or Rome and has his clothes handmade by the finest tailors of those great cities? He is precisely that wise and discriminating philologist who habituates Krüger's *Sprachlehre*[3] and the many contributions of the great American scholar to whom these essays are dedicated: that student of ancient syntax, who combined the acuteness and judgment of Krüger, the sensibility for nuance and idiom of Shilleto and Jebb, the historical sense of Wackernagel, and a style and perception of style that never fail to astonish and edify.

The tragedy is that we have no full-scale syntax from the master. The two parts of the *Syntax of Classical Greek* (henceforth *Syntax*) comprise only the doctrine of the simple sentence and the first part of the simple sentence expanded.[4] We lack treatment of oblique cases, prepositions, infinitive and participle, to mention only the main subjects that were to be treated next. (Our guide to these proposed contents is the *Latin Grammar*, first published in 1867.[5]) "In fact," writes Gildersleeve, "the Latin Syntax was based on the MS of the Greek."[6] I note in passing that though the *Syntax* did not reach the pronouns, Part II does contain the fullest (and I should say fundamental) treatment of the article known to me — the work, as Gildersleeve gratefully acknowledges, of Charles W. E. Miller, his co-worker in the *Syntax*.

We also lack treatment in this great fragment of subordinate clauses: object, purpose, result, causal, temporal, conditional, and concessive. Missing too are relative sentences, the arrangement of words and clauses, and the figures of syntax and rhetoric. (Imagine what this would have been!) To be sure, there is the magnificent series of articles, notes, and reviews in *AJP*, on which I paraphrase Goodwin from the preface to his *Moods* written in 1889.[7] From the sunlit shores of Lago Maggiore he informs us that "as editor of the *American Journal of Philology* [Gildersleeve] has discussed almost every construction of the Greek moods, and he has always left his mark." Two important review articles save us the trouble of reading a German monograph on the final sentence and contain much new and valuable material. "The acute observation, that the use of ἄν and κε in final constructions depends on the force of ὥς, ὅπως, and ὄφρα as conditional relative or temporal adverbs, explains much which before seemed inexplicable." Gildersleeve has "stated important principles of classic usage" of πρίν and "done much to correct current errors and to establish sounder views about [this conjunction]." Goodwin then goes on to laud work on the articular infinitive[8] and an article on the consecutive sentence[9] "which gives . . . the clearest statement ever made of the relations of ὥστε with the infinitive to ὥστε with the finite moods." The opinion expressed by the author of the standard work on Greek moods and tenses in English (and perhaps in any language) affirms that the disappointing lacunae in Gildersleeve's incomplete *Syntax* may be filled from the pages of *AJP* with some help from *TAPA*.

Again Gildersleeve and the whole of syntax may be partly glimpsed in the preface to his commentary on Pindar's *Pythian* and *Olympian Odes*.[10] The *Syntax* never reached oblique cases, but listen to the great man on the accusative *apud* the Boeotian: "The case-register of a poet is of especial importance for his style, and Pindar's use of the cases shows in an eminent degree his genius for vivid presentation. His free use of the accusative is a return to the original sweep of the case . . . the inner object has its wide poetic, its wide popular sweep."[11] Here thorough understanding of historical and descriptive syntax yields valuable insight into style. The comments on prepositions too offer much that illuminates matters of nuance and tone, Pindaric usage being frequently and instructively compared to that of prose.

On conditions also we are given considerably more than a mere set of rules: for example, Pindar's few ideal conditions are contrasted with the "narrow range" and "sharpness" of the poet's treatment of conditionals, "the predominance of the logical hypothesis, the indicative in protasis, the indicative or equivalent in apodosis": the "ideal conditions (εἰ with opt.) occur in dreamy, wistful passages, which seem to show that the optative is, after all, not ill-named."[12] Gildersleeve here enhances our perception of poetic attitude through syntactic observation.

An even better example is Gildersleeve on the Pindaric participle.

"It is natural," he tells us, "that the lyric poet should make large use of the participle, which enables him to concentrate his narrative on the main points, while preserving the color of the thought or description. . . . In narrative the participle gives color, gives atmosphere. Turn it into a finite verb and you have a catalogue, at best an outline, and not a picture."[13] The whole section merits close study with its analysis of the participle as an element in poetic narrative. Here one learns much that syntacticians Teutonic, Britannic, and North American seem rarely to perceive.

We have then a hint via Pindar of what the whole *Syntax* would have been. The wealth of material, information, and analysis that we do have in the two extant parts is astonishing enough; and again the perception and rendering of subtleties of nuance and tone command our wonder and admiration. The great wealth of examples also astonishes. The care and acuity with which they are selected, the originality of the selection—no mere dependence on Teutonic chalcoentery—all this makes the *Syntax* the great and indispensable work it is. Nor is a pungent and even Aristophanic sense of humor hidden from the careful reader. One such reader, as Professor William Calder reminds me, was R. W. Chapman, who noted the quotation at section 26 chosen to illustrate the forms of the subject in the simple sentence: τὸ παιδίον ἐβόα (Lysias 1.11), which Gildersleeve translates, "the baby was bawling."[14] Chapman calls this an example of Gildersleeve's sophisticated use of quotation: a wicked joke intended for the private ear of those familiar with Lysias' first speech; no one is insulted, and we are amused without offense.[15]

The massive recent interest in women's studies has made the passage alluded to as familiar as Astyanax's infant performance in *Iliad* 6. But just in case, I quote a modified version of Lamb's translation. The unsuspecting cuckold is speaking: "I came home unexpectedly from the country, and after dinner τὸ παιδίον ἐβόα ['The baby began to squall'—so Gildersleeve in section 205, p. 88] and behave peevishly, as the servant girl was annoying it on purpose to make it behave that way. For the fellow was in the house. I learned it all later." Gildersleeve gives us the baby at sections 26 (Forms of the Subject), 138 (The Active Voice), and 205 (The Imperfect Tense), where he translates "was squalling, began to squall, squalled." And we find Lysias 1.4, ὁ γὰρ ἄνθρωπος ἔνδον ἦν ("the fellow was within") at 62 (Copula as the Predicate) and 533 (Article with Objects Present to the Mind—appar-

ently Miller shared his senior colleague's sense of humor). Chapman's
acute observation is justified and amplified by the abovementioned data
taken from Peter Stork's immensely useful index compiled for the 1980
Dutch reprint of the *Syntax*.[16]

The Index also gives us valuable information about the authors
who passed under Gildersleeve's and Miller's scrutiny. In the Preface to
Part I, the former tells us, "Taking the Attic Orators as the standard of
conventional Greek, we have worked backward through philosophy and
history to tragic, lyric, and epic poetry, comedy being the bridge which
spans the syntax of the agora and the syntax of Parnassus."[17] (An acute
formulation of the comic world, not just the syntax of Aristophanes,
who by the way wins 13 columns in Stork, compared to 5, 9, and 8 for
Aeschylus, Sophocles, and Euripides, respectively.)

The total for oratory is a bit over 31 columns (almost 15 for Demosthenes). The clear winners are Homer with 20 and Plato with 19,
then come Xenophon, Thucydides, and Herodotus with 15, 14, and 13,
respectively. Among lyric and elegiac poets, Pindar has 6 and Theognis
9 — the master was apparently interested in complete works, not fragments or lecture notes. Poor Aristotle hasn't even a column, only four
entries. From this one can gauge the compilers' interests and, from the
reader's point of view, the kind of Greek he should turn to Gildersleeve's
*Syntax* for.

But there is of course much, much more than an authoritative account of the usage of these authors for the topics included in the two
parts of the *Syntax*. Comparison with standard commentaries is instructive here. First, the nominative in exclamations (Section 11), where
Gildersleeve is pitted against Page on *Medea* 61 and Jebb on *Philoctetes*
254. Jebb is silent; Page tells us simply that in exclamations the nominative, not the vocative, is the usual case. The master amplifies as follows:
"In exclamations, the nominative *characterizes*, the vocative *addresses*,
the accusative implies an *object of emotion*, and the genitive the *source
or sphere of emotion*."[18] A whole range of nuance is made clear at a
touch. Kühner, for his part, is content merely to note the usage.[19]

In section 198, Gildersleeve squares off against Barrett on *Hippolytus* 1060. The passage is, "Why am I not unsealing my lips?," which,
as Barrett paraphrases, is very nearly "I ought to unseal my lips."[20] (The
Greek is τί δῆτα τοὐμὸν οὐ λύω στόμα; [λύσω codd. : em. Elmsley]).
Barrett is copious and logical, as one expects. Gildersleeve is brief but
adds a telling point. The category he calls "Present in Passionate Ques-

tions"—his characterization is that "in passionate questions, the present is used as a form of exhortation."[21]

Comparison with Goodwin's *Moods* is also worth making. At stake is the translation of the potential optative. By reading the translation of the examples in Goodwin, section 244, one learns much about the range of meaning this usage is capable of. Gildersleeve discusses this range in a paragraph written with his usual clarity and sensitivity. I quote a few bits. "The optative with ἄν varies in tone from strong assurance (*must*) to faint presumption (*might*). *May be* is often a convenient rendering for the positive, *can't* for the negative. . . . So far from necessarily denoting uncertainty, it is the combination most frequently used to indicate moral certainty, and sometimes serves as a climax to the indicative."[22] (This last point one does not find *apud* the professor from Harvard.) Then follow copious examples, each translated with unfailing acuteness. Here too, clear arrangement explains much that is at best implied in Goodwin.

To conclude, I should like to note two observations made by Gildersleeve that seem especially noteworthy—though amidst such riches it is rash to single out any one thing. At section 405, *addenda* are given to the sections on the present and aorist imperative. Here we read that "the present imperative often produces the effect of an action that is watched."[23] The cooking scene from *Acharnians* (lines 1005 ff.) is cited as well as two passages from *Peace*, where instructions are given for preparing a bath, a bed, and a sacrifice (842 ff., 960 ff.). This is contrasted to a prayer in the same play (987 ff.). Here we see at a glance what we learn from the patient reading of some 140 pages of Bakker's *The Greek Imperative*.[24]

Finally, I cite the master on the subjunctive, which he calls "the mood of anticipation": "It anticipates the realization of the predicate, which anticipation appears chiefly as an act of the will."[25] A brilliant formulation to which is added the following: "Anticipation and expectation are not to be confounded. Anticipation treats the future as if it were present. Expectation postpones the realization. To anticipate payment and to expect payment are by no means the same thing, even in popular parlance, and grammarians should be at least as exact as the ungrammatical herd."[26] It appears that today the herd has sunk to the level of grammarians, who with a few exceptions can hardly hope to approach, much less match the genius for syntax so amply revealed by one of the greatest American scholars of classical Greek.

# NOTES

[1]R. Kühner and B. Gerth, *Ausführliche Grammatik der griechischen Sprache. Zweiter Teil: Satzlehre*[3] 2 vols. (Hannover and Leipzig 1898; reprint Darmstadt 1963).

[2]W. W. Goodwin, *Syntax of the Moods and Tenses of the Greek Verb*[2] (Boston 1890).

[3]K. W. Krüger *Griechische Sprachlehre für Schule*[4-6] (Leipzig 1875–1894), 2 parts in four volumes revised by W. Pökel.

[4]*Gildersleeve 3*.

[5]B. L. Gildersleeve and G. Lodge, *Gildersleeve's Latin Grammar*[3] (London and New York 1895) vii–x ("Contents"). The third edition was frequently reprinted and is the most accessible.

[6]*Gildersleeve 3*, I, iii.

[7]Goodwin, op. cit., viii–ix.

[8]"Contributions to the History of the Articular Infinitive," *TAPA* (1878) 5–19.

[9]"The Consecutive Sentence in Greek," *AJP* 7 (1886) 161–75.

[10]*Gildersleeve 1*, section IX, lxxxvii–cxv. For the relation between generic syntax (of which the item just cited is a miniature example) and the development of the *Syntax*, see in this volume, Fowler, pp. 89–91.

[11]Ibid., lxxxviii–lxxxix.

[12]Ibid., cvi–cvii.

[13]Ibid., cix.

[14]*Gildersleeve 3*, I, 9.

[15]R. W. Chapman, *The Portrait of a Scholar and Other Essays Written in Macedonia 1916–1918* (Oxford 1920; reprint Freeport 1968) 85.

[16]See *Gildersleeve 3* in Bibliography.

[17]*Gildersleeve 3*, I, iv.

[18]Ibid., 3.

[19]Kühner, I, 46.

[20]W. S. Barrett, *Euripides Hippolytos* (Oxford 1964) 359.

[21]*Gildersleeve 3*, I, 85.

[22]Ibid., 176.

[23]Ibid., 160.

[24]W. F. Bakker, *The Greek Imperative* (Amsterdam 1966).

[25]*Gildersleeve 3*, I, 147.

[26]Ibid., n. 1.

# GILDERSLEEVE, *THE JOURNAL*, AND PHILOLOGY IN AMERICA[1]

(An Appreciation on the completion of 100 volumes of *AJP*)

George A. Kennedy

The nineteenth century saw two contrasting movements in classical studies in America. Although Greek and Latin continued to be widely taught in schools and colleges, their relevance for Americans was also increasingly questioned. It was a time of nationalism, agrarian democracy, and industrialism, which increasingly emphasized technology and ceased to find that "useful learning" in the classics that had been evident to John Adams or Thomas Jefferson at the founding of the Republic. At the same time, evangelical Christianity rejected the paganism of the classics, and romantic aesthetics replaced classical forms in architecture and the other arts.

One of the major objections to study of the classics by serious thinkers in nineteenth century America was the superficiality of the teaching of Greek and Latin. Charles Francis Adams, Jr., in 1883 doubted that among all the graduates of Harvard College, ten could read Greek or Latin despite the requirements in both languages.[2] Emphasis was often on rote memorization of words and forms, with little understanding by teacher or student of either the grace of the languages or the meaning of the literatures. A second movement evident in the nineteenth century may be viewed at least in part as an attempt to meet these objections: this is the development of advanced studies and the birth in America of a humanistically directed study of philology. Beginning in 1815, and increasingly by the middle of the century, young Americans began to go off to study in German universities, which had emerged into international visibility as centers of learning and of science, and to return with dreams of encouraging a more profound study of the classics at home. One of those who went was Basil Lanneau Gildersleeve, and among the results of this interest was the foundation of the Johns Hopkins University in 1876 and of the *American Journal of Philology* in 1880, together with the establishment in the last decades of the century of graduate schools at many American universities and of schools of classical studies in Athens and in Rome.

Plans for the *American Journal of Philology*, as for learned journals in chemistry and mathematics, began soon after Gildersleeve's arrival at Hopkins, and the first, somewhat delayed, issue appeared early in 1880. In a brief "Retrospect" twenty-five years later, Gildersleeve told something of the *Journal's* birth pangs and of how he frequently had to put together a quick article himself to fill an issue when a promised contribution failed to arrive.[3] "In the early volumes," he said, was to be found "a certain grimness of resolve," but the *Journal* quickly earned serious attention on both sides of the Atlantic. It was intended to fill three major needs of the time, in which it had no American competitor. First, it was to provide a vehicle for dissemination on a quarterly basis of the best American scholarship on philology, which included Indic, Germanic, English, and Romance philology as well as classical, until various other publications were able to take over those fields. As such it was "not to be a Hopkins organ . . .; it was to be a national magazine . . . and as befits the liberal character of American institutions it was to be, if possible, an international magazine," open also to contributions from foreign scholars.[4] Second, there were to be regular "Reports" on the contents of European philological journals, many of which were not available in American libraries. This feature continued until 1935, by which time holdings in college libraries were judged adequate for most research. And there were to be substantial reviews, by experts in the field, of important new scholarly works. In addition to his full length articles, Gildersleeve began to contribute "Brief Mention" in 1884, his entertaining, highly literate, rather personal reaction to new books and developments in the field. He continued these contributions until 1920, and the best of them were subsequently collected by his successor as editor, Charles William Emil Miller, and published in 1930 as *Selections from the Brief Mention of Basil Lanneau Gildersleeve*, together with a biographical sketch and a list of publications, making a volume of over five hundred pages.

Gildersleeve's interests went well beyond the narrow limits of philology. Not only was philology to him a central part of the humanities, but he identified himself with the Old South and became an eloquent spokesman for the educational and literary development of the region, both before and after the war. It was in this role that the *Atlantic Monthly* asked him in 1891 to write the articles which were later (1915) republished together as *The Creed of the Old South*. His general view was that the South had a distinctive culture with strong literary appreciation and humanistic values and that the War Between the States was forced on the South by Northern autocracy, that it was fought by the Confederacy in the name of freedom over constitutional issues, and that the Southern states were rapidly approaching the abolition of slavery in their own way, which would have been accomplished without the war.

In 1915 Gildersleeve retired as Francis White Professor of Greek, but continued to edit the *Journal*. After 1916, in failing health and eyesight, he took less active part, but remained its chief editor through volume 40 (1919). He survived until his ninety-third year, amusing himself by writing sonnets, and died on January 9, 1924. On his deathbed he is supposed to have been asked where he wanted to be buried and to have replied, "Take me back to Charlottesville; I was dead there for twenty years."

Gildersleeve was an early member of the American Philological Association and served as its President in 1878 and again in 1909. His Presidential Address for 1878, expanded for publication in the *Princeton Review* the following year and reprinted in his *Essays and Studies* of 1890, is the Charter of American classical scholarship. The title is "University Work in America and Classical Philology," and it still deserves reading by members of the profession.

Although Gildersleeve in his address does not specifically define the goals of advanced study of the classics, his philosophy is clear from such statements as the following:

> While special research has, it is true, the drawback that it tends to make the course of instruction less symmetrical, what is lost in the rounded completeness of form is more than made up by the kindling of life that goes forth from every one who is engaged in the ardent quest of truth; and so thoroughly correlated is all knowledge, that there are subtle lines of connexion between the most remote regions of scientific study which vitalize theme and method through the whole intervening space.[5]

In speaking of the loss of "rounded completeness of form," Gildersleeve doubtless had in mind the *enkyklios paideia* of the Greeks and its medieval and modern development into the liberal arts of undergraduate education. He was well aware of the dangers of specialization and repeatedly warned against them, but he also thought that truth is essentially one, and the more of it is perceived, the more the relation, the value, and the meaning of the parts are laid open to the mind. His own great love was syntax, and he saw in it a parallel to the interconnected structure of all knowledge. On the tenth anniversary of the founding of Hopkins in 1886 he said,

To me, as an ardent lover of literature, as one who was led through literature to grammar and not through grammar to literature, the fairest results of a long life of study have been the visions of that cosmic beauty which reveals itself when the infinitely little fills up the wavering outlines and the features stand out pure and perfect against the sky of God's truth.[6]

Gildersleeve thought that university work in America should be American or, as he put it, "meet the needs of our civilization and bear the stamp of our national character." In his Presidential Address he asks what Americans do best and what they are least disadvantaged in doing, considering the slender library and museum resources of the time and the distance to the scenes of classical civilization.[7] He suggests five areas for American scholars to cultivate.

First, they can work closely and directly with texts and cognate original sources, read in context.[8] "If close acquaintance with the sources become the great characteristic of our philology, American books will receive higher approval from foreign critics than the half-pitying commendation with which they receive the faithful use of the most recent German works on the subjects treated."[9]

Second, "American scholars need not be shut out from their share in the positive gain to be derived from the newly-discovered inscriptions and monuments, which are adding more and more definiteness to our conception of the antique world and helping us to a better understanding of the dialectic life of the classic languages, and the cantonal and provincial life of the classic peoples."[10] It might be noted that the Archaeological Institute of America was founded the following year and the American School of Classical Studies at Athens three years later.

Third, "ancient history has to be interpreted into terms of American experience, and it would not be saying too much to maintain that many of the aspects of American life enable us to understand the ancients better than some of our European contemporaries can do."[11] He goes on to elaborate a view of the American as audacious, inventive, and ready-witted in ways not characteristic of the "pedantic" German, the "sceptical" English, and the "erratic" French. Some of these worthies subsequently protested at his characterizations.

Fourth, he says, "It is my firm conviction that the exact study of function will lead to valuable results in aesthetics as well, that the comparative study of syntax and the historical study of syntax are destined to give us a firmer foundation and a clearer outline for the whole structure of style than would have been thought possible some years ago."[12]

And fifth, lexicography. "The history of words or constructions is seldom so much as sketched, and the vast department of synonyms, which must be approached by each nationality from its own basis, is almost untouched in English."[13]

Gildersleeve was already looking forward to the *American Journal of Philology* when he spoke these words in 1878, and they foreshadow his policy as an editor. In the course of a century, the *Journal* has published distinguished contributions in all five areas, but the disciplines did not develop with the same speed. Henry T. Rowell, as editor on the occasion of the seventy-fifth anniversary of the *Journal*, undertook an interesting survey of its history and changing emphases.[14] The early issues, as he points out, are predominantly philological in a narrow sense, and we may say that they fall primarily within the fourth and fifth of Gildersleeve's five areas of research. His own article, "On the Stylistic Effect of the Greek Participle,"[15] is an excellent example of how syntax can be made to contribute to an understanding of style. The first area, the close study of texts, especially in a literary sense, emerged rather slowly, but is strong in the *Journal* by the beginning of the new century. Epigraphy, the second area, appears by volume 5 and has had a distinguished part in the *Journal*, including the editorship of Benjamin D. Meritt for five volumes. Ancient history, the third area, was slow in developing, but the arrival of Tenney Frank at Hopkins greatly accelerated its progress. He became editor for volumes 57 through 60. Frank clearly believed with Gildersleeve that American scholarship should have a distinctive point of view. In the preface to his first major work, *Roman Imperialism* (1914), he had taken issue with the doctrine that imperialism is the national expression of the individual's "will to live, . . . an axiom . . . too frequently assumed particularly in historical works that issue from the continent, where the overcrowding of population threatens to deprive the individual of his means of subsistence unless the united nation makes for itself a place in the sunlight."[16]

Frank goes on to say: "Let us imagine a people far removed from the economic pressure as well as the political traditions of modern Europe, an agricultural people, not too thickly settled, and not egged on by commercial ambitions, a republic in which the citizens themselves must vote whether or not to proclaim a war," and he describes a Rome not too different from America of the nineteenth century as seen by a Kansas farmer. It is relatively common to try to use the experience of antiquity as a way of understanding modern events. Frank and Gildersleeve did so occasionally, but were also moved by scholarly goals to use their experience of the modern world as a way of coming to a deeper understanding of ancient experience. In Frank's case, his insights into Roman agriculture and economics; in Gildersleeve's case, the great example is "A Southerner in the Peloponnesian War," an essay in which his own experiences in the Confederate cavalry and as a resident of Virginia during the War Between the States are transmuted into an understanding of Thucydides and what it would have been like to have lived in Greece during the Peloponnesian War.[17]

Gildersleeve is one of three to have been elected to a second term as president of the American Philological Association. This came in 1909, and an abstract of his address on that occasion can be found in the *Proceedings* of the Association.[18] His mood is expansive and triumphant.

> How needless now the preaching of the Presidential Address of 1878, how ample the fulfillment of the prophecy. . . . There are those whose ideal of America is a cosmopolitan blend of the best in all the varied nationalities, the thoroughness and grasp of the German, the sound sense of the English, the delicate literary touch of the French [he has modified his rhetoric a little]; and perhaps the peculiar character of our scholarship lies not so much in any one feature as in the hospitable acceptance and ready assimilation of whatever makes for life in the philological world; and it is this quickness to appreciate, this eagerness to assimilate, this openmindedness, "this clear vision and straight thought" that may be set down as specifically American, and as lending to all our work a truly national stamp.

The same year he returned to Charlottesville to give three lectures in the Barbour-Page Foundation series.[19] In these lectures, which bear more than the usual stamp of his energy and wit, he distinguishes three channels of life binding us to the Greeks. One is the continuous tradition of Greece from ancient to modern times in so far as it is a continuity. The second is the direct influence, conscious or unconscious, of Greek language and literature on English and American language and literature, especially of the nineteenth and twentieth century. The third is the affinity of Greek and American life, in which he takes up some of the concepts mentioned already, such as the understanding to be achieved of Thucydides from the circumstances of Virginia in 1864. Incidentally, Gildersleeve might not have approved of an historian of rhetoric as his eulogist. *Hellas and Hesperia* contains a characteristic epigram: "it is better to be a doorkeeper in the house of philology than to dwell in the tents of the rhetoricians."[20]

In 1919, on its fiftieth anniversary, the American Philological Association invited a series of papers on various aspects of the classics in the half-century. That on the history of the Association, by Frank Gardner Moore of Columbia, repeatedly refers to Gildersleeve. That on fifty years of classical studies in America was by Paul Shorey of Chicago, and it ends with a fine rhetorical syncrisis, the comparison of the three great models of turn of the century scholarship.[21] The model of British scholarship chosen is R. C. Jebb, author of great books on the Attic orators, on Homer, and on Greek poetry, as well as editor of Bacchylides and Sophocles. "In the virtuosity of scholarship," Shorey claims, "Jebb is easily first, not only in this group but of all European scholars since the Renaissance." That judgment, after another fifty years, would not be unanimously accepted, but still might be defended, just as Jebb's *Sophocles*, for all changing taste and improved knowledge, still survives as the greatest edition of the greatest Greek dramatist. The model taken for German scholarship is Wilamowitz, a figure about whom Shorey was always able to control his enthusiasm: "His mistakes"—and Shorey has in mind textual emendations and reasoning, built on misunderstanding of the text—"are at least proportionate to the number of stimulating suggestions he has put forth." And finally the model of the American scholar:

> Gildersleeve is one of us and perhaps too near and dear for impartial measurement. But as his *Pindar* might have said had he used the Whitmanian dialect of the American language, Gildersleeve's achievements make it a safe bet for his encomiast to yawp it over the roofs of the world that most of the men in this room have learned more Greek from him than from the other two scholars taken together, and that if his scattered and too often overlooked work could be collected and systematized[,] the tomes of Wilamowitz would not outweigh it in any judicious scales. To say nothing of the wit, wisdom, and eloquence of the wide-ranging "Essays and Studies," those who "never had a chance to see his notes on Justin Martyr," who have not read the text and translated the notes of his *Pindar* with successive classes, who have not compared his Latin Grammar with other mechanical compilations, who have not kept up with Brief Mention for the past forty years, have no conception of the stores of helpful and pregnant suggestion cached in these depositories. In sheer insight into the structure and genius of the Greek language he has no equal. . . . No, if we are to be judged by our leader we need fear no comparisons.[22]

All American scholars can take pride in Gildersleeve's leadership and in the accomplishments of the *Journal* under a succession of worthy editors: Miller, Meritt, Frank, Cherniss, Rowell, and Luck. We congratulate *AJP* on its centenary and pledge our support for the second century.

# NOTES

[1]Originally published in a slightly different form in *AJP* 101 (1980) 1-11.

[2]See *A College Fetich. An Address Delivered before the Harvard Chapter of the Fraternity of the Phi Beta Kappa* (Boston 1883) 16.

[3]"Retrospect," *AJP* 25 (1904) 486-90.

[4]Ibid.

[5]*Gildersleeve 2*, 92.

[6]"On the Present Aspect of Classical Study," *JHU Circulars* (June 1886) 106 (=*Gildersleeve 2*, 506).

[7]"University Work in America and Classical Philology," *Princeton Review* 55 (May 1879) 511-36 (=*Gildersleeve 2*, 87-123).

[8]Ibid., 519-23 (99-104).

[9]Ibid., 523 (104).

[10]Idem, (105).

[11]Idem.

[12]Ibid., 524 (106-7).

[13]Ibid., 525 (108).

[14]"Seventy-Five Years of the *AJP*," *AJP* 75 (1954) 337-58.

[15]*AJP* 9 (1888) 137-57.

[16](New York 1914) vii-ix.

[17]Originally published in *Atlantic Monthly* 80 (Sept. 1897) 330-42, reprinted in *Gildersleeve 5*, 55-103. For further discussion, see George Kennedy, "A Southerner in the Peloponnesian War," *Southern Humanities Review, Special Issue "The Classical Tradition in the South"* (Auburn, AL 1977) 21-25.

[18]*TAPA* 40 (1909) xxxviii-xxxix.

[19]*Gildersleeve 4*.

[20]Ibid., 45.

[21]"Fifty Years of Classical Scholarship in America," *TAPA* 50 (1919) 33-61.

[22]Ibid., 59-60.

# GILDERSLEEVE AND THE STUDY OF ATTIC TRAGEDY

Seth L. Schein

To anyone familiar with Gildersleeve's work, it may seem that mine is a non-subject, since throughout his career he wrote very little on Aeschylus, Sophocles, and Euripides. But that is just my point: for whatever reasons, Gildersleeve, who of course knew the tragic texts intimately, avoided discussing them in print and apparently discouraged others from doing so. Writings which are today, at least in the United States, at the heart of Greek literary studies for both classical scholars and nonspecialist readers were almost completely neglected by the greatest and one of the most broadly humane of American classicists. In this paper I shall attempt briefly to document this surprising neglect, to suggest some possible reasons for it, and to consider its effect on American classical studies in Gildersleeve's lifetime and since then.

In his long career Gildersleeve neither edited a tragic text nor wrote a book on a tragic poet nor contributed a literary or historical study on a topic in Attic tragedy. His single philological article on a tragic topic, entitled, "On εἰ with the Future Indicative and ἐάν with the Subjunctive in the Tragic Poets," appeared in 1876[1]; he never contributed anything on Attic tragedy to his own *American Journal of Philology*, apart from his Brief Mentions. And even among his numerous Brief Mentions there are relatively few essays on Aeschylus, Sophocles, and Euripides until late in Gildersleeve's life, when he published more extended pieces on all three poets.[2]

Gildersleeve's reluctance to write on the tragic poets extended to his policy as editor. In the first forty volumes of *AJP*, beginning in 1880, there were fewer than twenty articles or notes on tragic subjects. Most of these were text-critical or dealt with the archaeology of the ancient theater and with ancient theater production. Charles Knapp's essay, "A Point in the Interpretation of the *Antigone* of Sophocles,"[3] was the *first* extended literary critical study of tragedy published in the *Journal*; it was followed two years later by two interpretive studies, "The Function and Dramatic Value of the Recognition Scene in Greek Tragedy," by D. C. Stuart, and "The 'Thought' Motif of Wisdom versus Folly in Greek Tragedy," by La Rue Van Hook (a response to Knapp).[4] *AJP*'s aversion to work on tragedy extended even to its book reviews. In the same forty years there were only about fifteen reviews by Gildersleeve and others of editions of plays and books on tragic topics, and many of the most important publications of the period passed without notice, including, for example, some of Jebb's editions of Sophocles' plays[5] and Wilamowitz's epoch-making *Herakles*.[6] In his Brief Mentions, Gildersleeve more than once expressed his admiration for the achievements of these scholars,[7] and others of Wilamowitz's books were reviewed in *AJP*,[8] but this did not earn either the first or revised edition of *Herakles* a review. *AJP* also neglected many of the finest American editions of Greek plays, for example the *Oedipus Tyrannus* and *Medea* of Mortimer Lamson Earle.[9] The only major exceptions to Gildersleeve's editorial policy were reviews of Lewis Campbell's edition of Sophocles by J. W. White and of Kaibel's edition of Sophocles' *Electra* by Gildersleeve himself.[10] This latter review was far more literary than most *AJP* pieces on tragedy and showed what Gildersleeve could do when he let himself go. In it, he quoted Matthew Arnold and emphasized the need for exhaustive literary interpretation before any radical attack on the text.[11] But this review stands out as an unparalleled anomaly during Gildersleeve's years as editor. It is perhaps no accident that the literary articles by Knapp, Stuart, and Van Hook, which I have mentioned, were published only after C. W. E. Miller had assumed joint editorial responsibility for the *Journal*.[12]

Gildersleeve's lack of interest in Attic tragedy as scholar and editor is in accord with his avoidance of the genre and its authors in his other, more popular writings.[13] When he mentions the tragedians at all, it is for the light they throw on history: "The Persian War," he says, "must be studied in Aeschylus as well as in Herodotus, the Peloponnesian in Euripides and Aristophanes as well as in Thucydides and Xenophon."[14] The Peloponnesian War was of particular interest to Gildersleeve, who saw analogies and repeatedly drew parallels between it and the Civil War. As he wrote in *Hellas and Hesperia*, referring to his service in the Confederate Army, "The period in which some of us lived most intensely, in which we lived on the highest level on which mortals can live, has its parallels in Thucydides' History of the War between the States."[15] He was interested in Thucydides and Aristophanes as "registering the experiences" of that war,[16] and in Euripides chiefly, it would seem, as a means to understanding Aristophanes.[17] It is no accident that, while Gildersleeve regularly taught Aristophanes and Thucydides in his years at Johns Hopkins, he never taught Aeschylus or Euripides, and he did not teach Sophocles once he had left the University of Virginia in 1876.[18] He confessed on several occasions to his "boyish enthusiasm for the lyric measures of the Greek tragic poets,"[19] but this enthusiasm did not affect his reluctance to teach these poets or to discuss them in print.

It is, of course, paradoxical at first glance that the editor of Pindar, whose sensitivity to poetry and ability to interpret it are apparent both from his edition of the *Olympian* and *Pythian Odes* and from the numerous translations and interpretive asides that flowed from his pen, should have so avoided the tragic poets — the only major authors of classical Greek literature in any genre whom he did avoid. It certainly was not a matter of ignorance; as I have said, he knew the tragic texts intimately, as he knew all Greek literature. His one article on conditional forms in the tragic poets showed his fine ability to discriminate among them accurately and sensitively, demonstrating how Euripides, unlike Aeschylus and Sophocles, puts the majority of his future conditions in the ἐάν form, thus approaching more closely than the other two the language of prose.[20] Furthermore, Gildersleeve used his understanding of Sophocles' characteristic plot structure, which he called "an artistic reproduction of the real working of human destinies," to describe imaginatively and eloquently the fatal career of the Emperor Maximilian of Mexico as a Sophoclean tragedy.[21]

I would suggest two possible reasons for Gildersleeve's reluctance to write about Attic tragedy: in the first place, he was attracted as much or more to exceptional *lives* as to outstanding literary works; this is clear from his essays on Apollonius of Tyana, Lucian, and the emperor Julian,[22] as well as from his scattered remarks on the lyric and tragic poets. But very little is known of the lives of the tragedians, and though Gildersleeve refers to such stories as that of Aeschylus' death and that of Sophocles as a youth leading the dance in celebration of the victory at Salamis, there clearly was little grist for his mill in the study of their plays. In the second place, and more importantly, throughout his writings Gildersleeve shows what I would call an aristocratic bias in favor of traditional institutions and values, traditional forms of heroic excellence. This preference is reflected in his wonderfully sympathetic introduction and commentary on the *Olympian* and *Pythian Odes* of Pindar, as well as by his appreciation of and loyalty to what he called "The Creed of the Old South," whose way of life he identified with that of oligarchical Sparta, just as he identified the Northern states with democratic Athens.[23] Perhaps Attic tragedy, a genre whose efflorescence was a product and historical concomitant of fifth century Athenian democracy, and which regularly revised or questioned traditional, aristocratic heroes, myths, institutions, and values in the light of modern intellectual and moral developments, could not have appealed to a man of Gildersleeve's experience, values, and temperament. It is worth noting that during World War I, when the traditional certainties and fundamental optimism of pre-war Europe and America were being shattered, *AJP* began to publish the interpretive articles on Attic tragedy to which I have referred, and Gildersleeve wrote his longer Brief Mentions on Aeschylus, Sophocles, and Euripides. The problematic, morally ambivalent, disturbing dramas by these poets must have seemed freshly relevant to him in an era of profound social and spiritual dislocation.

Because Gildersleeve was so dominant and influential a figure in American classics, his aversion to Attic tragedy was reflected in the work of his students and of American classicists generally. Few of the sixty-seven doctoral dissertations that he directed dealt with the tragic poets, and in their later scholarly careers his students likewise tended to avoid these authors.[24] Other journals followed the lead of *AJP* in publishing relatively few interpretive articles and reviews on tragedy. This may, in part, have been a function of the aims and methods of the *Altertumswissenschaft* then in fashion, which emphasized textual, historical, and biographical studies and had little or no interest in literary criticism. But in other cases Gildersleeve notoriously transcended the limitations of this dominant historical scholarship by his personal enthusiasm, his subjective value judgments, and the idiosyncratic style and manner in which he expressed his views. The question remains, Why did he not do so in the case of Attic tragedy? Apart from what I have already suggested, I know of no solution to this problem.

One legacy of Gildersleeve's disinclination was the relative paucity of books and articles on the tragic poets by American scholars all the way through the 1920s, '30s, and '40s. Only after World War II, which stimulated work on Attic tragedy for much the same reasons as World War I had, and after the absorption by American scholars of much of the best continental research of the previous two decades, did we begin to break out of the *de facto* restriction on the literary study of tragedy which had been largely the result of Gildersleeve's taste and influence. Even today, relatively few of our Hellenists specialize in the tragic poets, although to scholars of other languages and literatures and to the "common reader," the study of Greek tragedy is one of the chief glories of our discipline, one of the main things classics is about.

I hope I shall not seem to have disparaged Gildersleeve, whose scholarship and personality I find continually instructive and inspiring, because of his relative neglect of Attic tragedy. I have simply tried to call attention to his surprising lack of professional interest in the genre, and to the historical effect of this lack of interest on American classical scholarship. Perhaps the realization that the traditional avoidance of literary critical studies of the tragedies has been largely a legacy of one man's taste and influence will help to stimulate more and better interpretations of these plays in the future.

# NOTES

[1]*TAPA* 7 (1876) 5–23.

[2]His longest essay on Aeschylus is his review of Wilamowitz's *Aischylos*, *AJP* 36 (1915) 358–69 (=*Gildersleeve 6*, 332–38); cf. his notes on translations of Aeschylus, at 23 (1902) 467–70 (=*Gildersleeve 6*, 85–88) and on Verrall's *Choephori*, 14 (1893) 398 (=*Gildersleeve 6*, 20–21). On Sophocles, see 39 (1918) 99–101 (=*Gildersleeve 6*, 382–86); and on Euripides, see 36 (1915) 230–36 (=*Gildersleeve 6*, 320–27), 37 (1916) 370–78 (=*Gildersleeve 6*, 356–63).

[3]*AJP* 37 (1916) 300–16.

[4]Stuart, ibid., 39 (1918) 268–90; Van Hook, ibid., 393–401.

[5]But cf. Gildersleeve at *AJP* 17 (1896) 390: "the most considerable edition of Sophokles in English—it might be safe to say in any language—is complete." See also, ibid., 39 (1918) 99 (=*Gildersleeve 6*, 382).

[6]*Euripides Herakles*, 2 vols. (Berlin 1889; Berlin 1909²).

[7]On Jebb, see *AJP* 28 (1907) 479–82 (=*Gildersleeve 6*, 148–51) and ibid., 39 (1918) 99–100 (=*Gildersleeve 6*, 382–83); on his individual books, see ibid., 10 (1889) 123–24; 15 (1894) 118–19; 28 (1907) 479; 17 (1896) 390 (see also 30 [1909] 226), as well as his memorial notice, 26 (1905) 491. On Wilamowitz, see 13 (1892) 517–18 (*Hippolytus*); 16 (1893) 125 (*Aristotles und Athen*); 22 (1901) 231 and 34 (1913) 109–11, 232 (*Reden und Vorträge*); 27 (1906) 357 (*Griechische Literatur*); 33 (1912) 361–63 (*Mimnermos und Propertius*). Gildersleeve reviewed *Bucolici Graeci* in 27 (1906) 336–41. The next book of Wilamowitz to be reviewed in *AJP* was *Die Ilias und Homer* in 42 (1921) 274–80, by G. M. Bolling.

[8]See notes 2 and 7 above.

[9]*The Oedipus Tyrannus of Sophocles* (New York 1901); *The Medea of Euripides* (New York 1904).

[10]*AJP* 3 (1882) 94–97; ibid., 18 (1897) 353–56. Gildersleeve also reviewed Wheeler's *De Alcestidis et Hippolyti Euripidearum interpolationibus* 1 (1880) 72–73, F. W. Schmidt's *Kritische Studien zu den griechischen Dramatikern*, 10 (1889) 87–91, Ridgeway's *The Origin of Tragedy*, 32 (1911) 210–15, and Robert's *Oidipus*, 36 (1915) 338–44.

[11]"Exhaust interpretation before you attack the text," 353.

[12]Miller became associate editor in 1916, but Gildersleeve remained chief editor until 1920. See H. T. Rowell, "Seventy-Five Years of the 'A.J.P.,'" *AJP* 75 (1954) 341.

[13]But see, in *The Nation*: "The 'Agamemnon' at Oxford," June 24, 1880, 472–73; "The 'Oedipus Tyrannus' at Harvard," May 19, 1881, 347–48, "The Agamemnon of Aeschylus," *New Eclectic Magazine* 6 (June 1870) 675–77.

[14]"The Limits of Culture," *Southern Review* 2 (1867) 433 (=*Gildersleeve 2*, 19). In this essay and in "Classics and Colleges," *Princeton Review* 54 (1878) 67-95 (=*Gildersleeve 2*, 43-84), Gildersleeve twice quoted with approval John Stuart Mill's statement that "all that is left to us of ancient historians, orators, philosophers, and even dramatists, are replete with remarks and maxims of singular good sense and penetration, applicable both to political and private life" (435-36 and 69, respectively [=*Gildersleeve 2*, 22 and 47]); but in each case Mill omits the tragic poets from a list of "the acute and observing minds of those ages," the authors whose "rich store of experience of human nature and conduct" make them important for students of classics.

[15]*Gildersleeve 4*, 47-48.

[16]Ibid., 124.

[17]*AJP* 36 (1915) 230 (=*Gildersleeve 6*, 321). On Euripides as a poet, see ibid., 31 (1910) 359 (=*Gildersleeve 6*, 205-6).

[18]Ibid., 37 (1916) 373 (=*Gildersleeve 6*, 357); cf. 39 (1918) 99 (=*Gildersleeve 6*, 382).

[19]Ibid., 36 (1915) 361 (=*Gildersleeve 6*, 336).

[20]See n.1 above and in this volume, Vaio, p. 37.

[21]"Maximilian: His Travels and His Tragedy," *Southern Review* 3 (1868) 476-505 (=*Gildersleeve 2*, 453-96); the words quoted appear on 476 (=*Gildersleeve 2*, 454).

[22]See *Gildersleeve 2*, 249-96, 297-351, 353-98.

[23]*Gildersleeve 5*; cf. *Gildersleeve 4*, 94.

[24]Those who wrote dissertations on tragic topics were Gonzalez Lodge, *The Participle in Euripides* (1886); James Thomas Lees, Δικανικὸς λόγος *in Euripides* (1889); Henry Rushton Fairclough, *The Attitude of the Greek Tragedians toward Nature* (1896); Herbert Baldwin Foster, *On the Significance of the Deus ex Machina in the Extant Dramas of Euripides* (1900); Ashton Waugh McWhorter, *The Effect of Person on Mood: . . . in Aeschylus, Sophocles, and Euripides* (1905); and Thomas Wyatt Dickson, *Compound Words in the Tragic Poets, Attic Orators, and Plato* (1913).

# GILDERSLEEVE IN AMERICAN LITERATURE: THE "KALEIDOSCOPIC STYLE"

## E. Christian Kopff

"My early ambition was to become a man of letters," Basil Lanneau Gildersleeve wrote in a Brief Mention in the *American Journal of
Philology* in 1904. "My monument was to have been the Greek Life of
the Second Century after Christ. But life shapes itself in its own way. I
have become a grammarian and my monument is to be the Monte Tes-
taccio of a philological journal."[1] Gildersleeve never wrote his monument, a single Great Work, but his style secured for him a position in
the American literature of his day that was recognized by such figures as
William P. Trent, in his then standard *History of American Literature*,
and Albert Jay Nock, in his *Theory of Education in the United States*,[2]
the greatest of the Page-Barbour Lectures, which are given at the University of Virginia, a series inaugurated by Gildersleeve.

Gildersleeve wrote essays and delivered speeches, as he studied
Greek, for most of his adult life. When he made a selection of his earlier
work for republication in *Essays and Studies, Educational and Literary*,[3] he included eight pieces from the *Southern Review* of 1867–1869
and a few later pieces from the *Princeton Review* from 1877, 1878, and
1883, along with a few Hopkins addresses. He did not at the time reprint his essays, "On the Steps of the Bema: Studies in the Attic Orators,"[4] although he envisioned its re-working for a republication which
never ensued.[5] As readable as many of these pieces are, they form only
the preamble to the prose of the quarter-century from 1885–1910, when
he published the "Introductory Essay" to his school edition of Pindar
(1885), the essays in the *Atlantic*, which he later reprinted as *The Creed
of the Old South* (1915), the Page-Barbour Lectures, *Hellas and Hesperia* (1909), and his great answer to Wilamowitz on Pindar, "The Seventh Nemean Revisited" (1910).[6] Throughout this period and after,
there are many thoughtful and witty pages contributed to the Brief
Mention section of *AJP* and many talks and addresses, some of which
were published.[7] Taken together, this represents a considerable body of
work, written in an individual and uniquely American style.

Let me analyze some characteristics of this style, quote a few brief
examples, and then comment on the style's future and significance.

Gildersleeve's sentences are usually long, but there is little feeling of Ciceronian periodicity. On the contrary, they are leisurely and conversational. The language moves at a dignified pace, but with an urgent staccato quality playing in the background. The most obvious reason for this last trait is Gildersleeve's use of asyndeton, omission of the connective (especially "and"), a trait that increased with the years. Despite the frequent asyndeton, whenever there is danger of obscurity or unseemly haste, anaphora, repetition, appears, to slow down or to clarify.

The conversational quality is accentuated by the common interplay of high language and low. Most familiar to the student of American literature from the prose of Henry James, the poetry of Pound and Eliot, we find this very modern trait in full bloom in the prose of the old Southern scholar. As in the poetry of Eliot and Pound, however, this conversational quality is tempered by the constant play of allusion. Gildersleeve defended his constant quoting and alluding thus: "If the surface meaning is perfectly plain, the cryptic meaning adds for the initiated a peculiar charm, not a vulgar wink, but a half-smile, a narrowing of the eyelids — a favorite contention of mine."[8] The literature of Greece and Rome, of England, France, Italy, and Germany, the Scriptures themselves, play a continual game of hide-and-go-seek through whatever subject the stylist is discoursing on. We hear always the accents of an individual voice, speaking, however, from a depth of wisdom and experience which only prolonged contact with the great minds of the past can bring. The often very American subject matter glitters and sparkles with the gems of a half-dozen languages and many centuries.

It is this interplay of languages and levels within one language that gives to Gildersleeve's style the character which he himself described as "kaleidoscopic."[9] It can be pedantic and precise, or wild and suggestive; very learned and international, or very familiar and American. Students of English may be grateful that Gildersleeve wrote English and not Latin. "Latin, any kind of Latin, would check the hypertrophy of psychological syntax and make the antics of *Brief Mention* next to impossible."[10]

Let me quote first from the famous passage from the "Introductory Essay" to Pindar, in which Gildersleeve defended and explained Pindar's attitude during and after the Persian Invasion — and by inference his own during and after the War Between the States·

In the sense that he loved all Greece, that he felt the ties of blood, of speech, above all, the ties of religion, Pindar was Panhellenic. The pressure of the barbarian that drew those ties tighter for Greece generally, drew them tighter for him also; but how? We are in danger of losing our historical perspective by making Pindar feel the same stir in the same way as Aischylos. If he had, he would not have been a true Theban; and if he had not been a true Theban, he would not have been a true Greek. The man whose love for his country knows no local root, is a man whose love for his country is a poor abstraction; and it is no discredit to Pindar that he went honestly with his state in the struggle. It was no treason to Medize before there was a Greece, and the Greece that came out of the Persian War was a very different thing from the cantons that ranged themselves on this side and on that of a quarrel which, we may be sure, bore another aspect to those who stood aloof from it than it wears in the eyes of moderns, who have all learned to be Hellenic patriots. A little experience of a losing side might aid historical vision. That Pindar should have had an intense admiration of the New Greece, should have felt the impulse of the grand period that followed Salamis and Plataia, should have appreciated the woe that would have come on Greece had the Persians been successful, and should have seen the finger of God in the new evolution of Hellas — all this is not incompatible with an attitude during the Persian War that those who see the end and do not understand the beginning may not consider respectable.[11]

If at times, especially in Gildersleeve's later years, we may think that he can discourse on no subject without introducing Pindar, it is well to remember that he could no more speak on Pindar without introducing modern America and himself. "My life has been written *boustrophedon* fashion," he told his Virginia audience, "and as I turn the furrow, the Greek line can't be distinguished from the American."[12] This, too, lies behind much of the vivacity of his style and behind its depth. The ripples from the pebbles cast into time's river reverberate. Even a hasty reader can note the movement, but only a slow and careful perusal can detect whence and whither the ripples flow.

A good example of this consciousness, and of his allusiveness as well, comes from the "Introductory Essay," where he evokes Dante to help elucidate a passage in Pindar:

> In the second Olympian he is telling of the blessedness of the souls that have overcome. When he comes to the damned, he calls them simply "those." "The others bear anguish too great for eye to look at." *Non ragioniam di lor.*[13]

The quotation from the passage in the *Commedia* where Virgil says to Dante, "Let us not speak of them," the Laodiceans whose lukewarmness makes them fit neither for Heaven or Hell, may call up for the thoughtful reader all sorts of similarities and differences implicit in comparing the two great religious poets. Typically Gildersleeve blinks his half-smile at the initiated, but does not expatiate. For the true initiate, however, there is more. In the notes added to the reprinting of *The Creed of the Old South*, Gildersleeve notes, "General Lee always referred to the enemy as 'those people'. . . . and I thought of General Lee as well as of Dante when I wrote in my Introductory Essay to Pindar," the passage we have quoted.[14]

*The Creed of the Old South* is Gildersleeve's clearest and most moving writing, *Hellas and Hesperia* his most pleasantly digressive, but Gildersleeve was always most serious, most artistic when writing on Pindar. As failing eyesight was bringing his career to a close, near the end of the first decade of the twentieth century, Wilamowitz wrote a famous and influential essay on Pindar's Seventh Nemean (1908).[15] Gildersleeve decided to analyze it and answer it to show the great German Hellenist and the world the merits, the superiority of his own "synthetic" method of Pindaric criticism. He has written in 1905:

> Analysis is apt to become a wooden and mechanical thing. What it yields is a jointed doll, not a rhythmical statue. The true way is to rethink the poet's, the philosopher's work. It is far more valuable to reproduce on a smaller scale than it is to translate.[16]

Gildersleeve did not publish his rethinking of Pindar's Seventh Nemean together with his discussion of Wilamowitz's essay until 1910.[17] As scholarship it is ripe wine, aged with many years. It also represents the *ne plus ultra* of Gildersleeve's stylistic extravagances. What must Wilamowitz have thought of the following?[18]

> Τιμά is after all surer than κλέος. Ninny's tomb keeps Ninny's name alive. One remembers *Batti veteris sacrum sepulcrum* and takes a recess for Lesbia's kisses.

Or of the following, on the name of Eleithuia, who is invoked at the beginning of the ode:

> Joledeth is the Hebrew for Birth and she may have been a Jewess who changed her name after the fashion set forth in Zangwill's "Children of the Ghetto." But the Greeks may have thought of ἐληλυθυῖα as one of Usener's transparent, or if not transparent, translucent goddesses. She is a manner of Ὥρα, the woman's "hour," as it is called in Scripture. If she is not, 'tis a pity she is not a Ὥρα.

These "intolerable vivacities," as he once called them,[19] go hand in hand with an attention to detail and feeling for the artistic unity of the poem that help make "The Seventh Nemean Revisited" still one of the most satisfying attempts to come to grips with this difficult poem. We find ourselves disturbed, as Housman said of Arthur Platt, "to meet with a scholar who carried his levity, where others carry their gravity, on the surface, and was austere, where he might without offence or detection have been frivolous, in conducting the operations of his mind."[20]

Gildersleeve's style was distinctively American, constructed out of the flotsam and jetsam of centuries and nations, extravagant, staccato, urgent with the present, with actuality, he would have said, yet profoundly conservative and respectful of the past. "I too would plead for an honest American literature, a literature of the soil, but the classics are in a measure our home."[21] In the twentieth century, the desire to imitate France and England carried off American prose, as France and Germany carried off American painting and architecture and the defiantly extravagant traditionalism that gave us Penn Station in New York, and Gildersleeve's prose style disappeared before the International Style and Hemingway's prose.

It is important to remember that Gildersleeve could create a style so responsive to American patterns of speech and thought because he was profoundly provincial, because he was profoundly classical. His stylistic creativity, like his important role in creating the modern research university, was rooted in a profound conservatism. He knew it himself. There is no better discussion of the role of conservatism in creativity than the following passage from the "Introductory Essay":

> Pindar was born at Thebes, the head of Boeotia — Boeotia, a canton hopelessly behind the times, a slow canton, as the nimble Attics would say, a glorious climate for eels, but a bad air for brains. Large historical views are not always entertained by the cleverest minds, ancient and modern, transatlantic and cisatlantic; and the annals of politics, of literature, of thought, have shown that out of the depths of crass conservatism and proverbial sluggishness come, not by any miracle, but by the process of accumulated force, some of the finest intelligences, some of the greatest powers, of political, literary, and especially religious life. Modern illustrations might be invidious, but modern illustrations certainly lie very near.[22]

It is perhaps no accident that the two best examples of the kaleidoscopic style in our day are to be found in two extravagant mockers of Northern and Eastern pretensions, both raised in the South, both conservatives, Tom Wolfe and William F. Buckley, Jr. Basil Gildersleeve would not have been surprised. As our quotations show, he was well aware that the truly American is to be found in the truly provincial, that the richly creative may need the support of the pedantically classical.

## NOTES

[1]*AJP* 25 (1904) 357-58 (=*Gildersleeve 6*, 115).

[2]William P. Trent, *A History of American Literature. 1607–1865* (New York 1903 and often reprinted) 565, mentioned at *AJP* 25 (1904) 357-58, n. 1 (=*Gildersleeve 6*, 115, n. 1); Albert Jay Nock, *The Theory of Education in the United States* (New York 1932) 95.

[3]*Gildersleeve 2*.

[4]*Southern Magazine* 12 (n.s. 5) 395-404, 559-69, 664-71; 13 (n.s. 6) 4-22, 129-37, 272-83.

[5]*Gildersleeve 2*, third (unnumbered) page of introduction.

[6]"The Seventh Nemean Revisited," *AJP* 31 (1910) 125-33.

[7]There is a useful bibliography accompanying Miller's "Biographical Sketch" in *Gildersleeve 6*, xxx-liii.

[8]*AJP* 32 (1911) 483 (=*Gildersleeve 6*, 238).

[9]*AJP* 31 (1910) 109 (=*Gildersleeve 6*, 196).

[10]*AJP* 28 (1907) 232 (=*Gildersleeve 6*, 143).

[11]*Gildersleeve 1*, xii.

[12]*Gildersleeve 4*, 124.

[13]*Gildersleeve 1*, xxxviii. See Dante, *Inferno* III.49:

(Fama di loro il mondo esser non lassa:
Misericordia e giustizia gli sdegna.)
Non ragioniam di lor, ma guarda e passa.

[14]*Gildersleeve 5*, 109-10.

[15]Ulrich von Wilamowitz-Moellendorff, "Pindars siebentes nemeisches Gedicht," *SPAW* Nr. 15 (1908) 328-52.

[16]*AJP* 26 (1905) 359 (=*Gildersleeve 6*, 120). Gildersleeve had worked on the project before Wilamowitz's essay impelled him into publication.

[17]See note 6 above. The quotations that follow come from pp. 131 and 132.

[18]See in this volume, Fowler, p. 77.

[19]*Gildersleeve 2*, second (unnumbered) page of introduction.

[20]Preface to *Nine Essays* by Arthur Platt (Cambridge 1927) x (=*The Classical Papers of A. E. Housman*, 3, J. Diggle and F. R. D. Goodyear, eds. [Cambridge 1972] 1272).

[21]*Gildersleeve 4*, 70-71.

[22]*Gildersleeve 1*, viii.

# THE GILDERSLEEVE ARCHIVE[1]

Robert L. Fowler

Basil Lanneau Gildersleeve (1831-1924) was both a great scholar and a figure of the first importance in the history of American education. Prior to his call to the Johns Hopkins University in 1876 there did not exist in America an institution that could properly be called a university, that is, one promoting research both by its professors and by graduate students working toward the doctor's degree.[2] The Baltimore foundation was meant to be such an institution, and when its first president, Daniel Coit Gilman (1831-1908),[3] looked about for scholars capable of meeting its needs, he saw Gildersleeve, then with twenty years behind him at the University of Virginia. Gildersleeve was in fact the first professor to sign a contract.[4] He brought with him the ideals of German scientific scholarship, having obtained his doctorate from the University of Göttingen in 1853;[5] he also brought with him the German seminar, having learned its workings from the master, Friedrich Ritschl.[6] He set up a graduate department and started his seminar;[7] other departments at Hopkins followed suit, and other institutions followed Hopkins.[8] Gildersleeve may be called the *pater studiorum* not only of American classical scholars but of all scholars here, since, with Gilman, he actually transplanted the idea of a university from the soil where Wilhelm von Humboldt first conceived it.

It is amazing that up to recently very little attention has been devoted to him. A flurry of newspaper articles[9] and obituaries in the learned journals[10] when he died; his successor C. W. E. Miller's publication of *Selections from the Brief Mention of Basil Lanneau Gildersleeve* (1930); since then, nothing apart from an occasional reminiscence.[11] Of late, however, there have been signs of quickening interest, as the papers in this volume attest. William M. Calder III has recently published some important correspondence,[12] and in another location called for a biography of Gildersleeve;[13] so has G. A. Kennedy.[14]

The materials for a life of Gildersleeve are extensive. Published sources alone — foremost among them Gildersleeve's own autobiographical essays — give a very complete picture, especially for his later years.[15] There are also unpublished documents in small collections scattered around the Southern states, as far north as Ithaca, New York and Cambridge, Massachusetts, and as far west as San Marino, California. Many of these are valuable for the years before 1876.[16] But by far the biggest collection is, of course, in Baltimore.

The archive is housed in the Special Collections section of the Milton S. Eisenhower Library. The section has received attention recently and is undergoing modification and expansion. As regards Gildersleeve, a separate collection of documents, mostly pertaining to administrative affairs and previously housed in the University Archives, has been sent over to Special Collections, where the two lots are being amalgamated and recatalogued. The Department of Classics also had a certain amount of material in its possession, and this has been sent over to join the rest. The end result will be an archive of some 7500 items. It is a fantastic treasure.

It might be thought desirable to have available a complete description of the archive, but that is not possible here. The main purpose is to publish several important documents which emerged during a fortnight's study in June 1982. Nevertheless, it seemed useful to preface these documents with some kind of general description. In this way the attention of scholars could be brought to the true extent of this great collection, and any future investigator could at least save himself some time in orientation.[17] I shall begin, then, with such a description in Part I, taking the opportunity to dilate on a few items of special note. The documents are published in Part II.

## I. Description of the Archive

The material falls readily into the categories: correspondence; lectures; notebooks; books and offprints; diaries; miscellany.

*1. Correspondence.* By far the greatest part of the archive consists of a correspondence of over 7,000 letters, mostly dating to the period after 1876. The letters can easily be consulted in files according to addressee. There are also letters by or pertaining to Gildersleeve in other archives in Special Collections, such as the Gilman archive, where will be found, for example, correspondence of 1883-1884 concerning an attempt to attract to Baltimore the renowned Indo-European scholar Karl Brugmann.[18] There is relevant material also in the Leonard L. Mackall archive, especially Mackall's letters to C. W. E. Miller, as well as those to F. G. Allinson, who wrote the article on Gildersleeve for the *Dictionary of American Biography.* There is no danger of missing any of these letters since they are all well cross-indexed in the catalogue.

The leads contained in this correspondence could take a biographer to every corner of the world in search of documents. One circumstance will, however, assist him considerably. Gildersleeve was in the habit of making rough drafts of most of his letters, which he then kept for his records. Thus the archive contains, in a very large number of cases, both sides of a correspondence. Gildersleeve's drafts are usually very close to the final form of his letters, though not, of course, identical.

Apart from hundreds of letters to family members, there are many to now forgotten colleagues in Southern universities. As the letters will make the flesh of a biography, the putative author would need to be well versed in the history, not to say the ethos, of those institutions. There are also many correspondents well known to classical scholars. Among them: G. M. Bolling, C. D. Buck, S. H. Butcher, G. M. Calhoun, Edward Capps,[19] Lane Cooper, John Dewey,[20] J. Wight Duff, Robinson Ellis, H. R. Fairclough, Edward Fitch,[21] Tenney Frank, W. W. Goodwin, A. Gudeman, W. G. Hale, Edith Hamilton, J. Rendel Harris, G. L. Hendrickson, Oliver Wendell Holmes, Jr., E. Hübner,[22] Paul Kretschmer, W. Kroll,[23] G. M. Lane, Gonzalez Lodge, James Loeb,[24] C. W. E. Miller, W. A. Oldfather, A. C. Pearson, W. K. Prentice, E. K. Rand, D. M. Robinson, J. E. Sandys,[25] J. H. H. Schmidt,[26] Max Schneidewin,[27] J. A. Scott, T. D. Seymour, Paul Shorey,[28] E. G. Sihler, Charles Forster Smith, Kirby Flower Smith, H. W. Smyth, B. L. Ullman, Hermann Usener,[29] Johannes Vahlen,[29] B. I. Wheeler, John Williams White, Ulrich von Wilamowitz-Moellendorff,[29] Woodrow Wilson.[30] The correspondence with Lodge, Miller, Sihler, K. F. Smith, and White is extensive.

2. *Lectures*. Over thirty lectures survive, mostly in handwritten copies. Datable ones fall in the period between 1876 and 1907. The lion's share is claimed by Aristophanes, an author who took second place in Gildersleeve's heart only to Pindar. One bundle contains a course of public lectures delivered sometime after 1904, but incorporating earlier material; a second bundle contains two lectures dating to 1887 and one to 1897. Another lecture bears the inscription "Harvard Lecture no. 1," and two others are identifiable from a chart at the end of the second bundle just mentioned as also belonging to the Harvard tour of 1898. Three other lectures from that tour are missing. Two more lectures simply entitled "Aristophanes" are not precisely identifiable as to date or venue; one has a *terminus post quem* of 1907, and the other is a lecture he delivered to college seniors. These and other lectures in the collection give some idea of Gildersleeve in the flesh; the style is as exuberant and kaleidoscopic[31] as one might expect.[32]

Next in order comes Pindar. In the first year of the university's operation, Gildersleeve gave a course of public lectures on Greek lyric poetry. In the course there were four lectures on Pindar; all of these survive, together with one on "Hipponax, Fable, Babrius," and notes for three others. In these Pindaric lectures, many of the keynotes heard in the later commentary (1885) are clearly sounded.[33]

Other authors represented are Demosthenes and Thucydides (one lecture each); and there are general lectures on Greek tragedy, Greek philosophy, Greek prose literature, Greek history, and "H & C" (Hermeneutics and Criticism). It appears that the survival of these lectures was purely a matter of chance (for example, lectures numbers 2 and 3 on Greek history survive, but not number 1). Except for those on Aristophanes, all were found among the items possessed by the Classics Department — a large box of unsorted papers of the most miscellaneous nature.[34]

In addition to these complete lectures, there are fragmentary drafts, excerpts, and notes in many of the notebooks.

3. *Notebooks.* A great many notebooks contain a wealth of material. Most periods of Gildersleeve's life are represented. First, there are the notes he took as a student in Germany, 1850–1853. His impressions and experiences are referred to often in his writings; his diaries are also found in the archive (see below). The impact of these three years was, quite simply, overwhelming; it is no accident that he carefully preserved most of the records.[35]

The student notebooks number sixteen and include eighteen courses of lectures, which will be almost all that he heard.[36] His teachers included such luminaries as Jacob Bernays, August Böckh, J. Franz, K. F. Hermann, E. L. von Leutsch, Friedrich Ritschl, F. W. Schneidewin, and F. G. Welcker. All except Franz and Hermann are represented here,[37] and the potential for discovery is great for anyone interested in German intellectual history. Close study would, however, cost one some of his eyesight; Gildersleeve's cramped hand is difficult at the best of times, quite defeating when he is writing quick, heavily abbreviated German. Only one notebook (in two parts, Böckh's lectures on Demosthenes) is written in English. One (von Leutsch on Catullus and Propertius) is in Gothic script.

The important notebooks are: Bernays on Aristotle's *Poetics* (Bonn, Sommersemester 1852); the same on Thucydides (Bonn, Wintersemester 1852–1853); Böckh on Demosthenes, *De Corona* and on Greek literature (Berlin, WS 1850–1851); von Leutsch on Catullus and

Propertius (Göttingen, SS 1851); Ritschl on Aristophanes' *Frogs* and the history of Greek comedy, and on "Kritik und Hermeneutik" (Bonn, SS 1852); the same on Plautus, and "Encyclopädie der Philologie" (Bonn, WS 1852–1853); Schneidewin on Greek lyric poetry except Pindar (Göttingen, WS 1851–1852); and Welcker on the history of Greek art (Bonn, SS 1852). From these I single out Ritschl's lectures on "Encyclopädie der Philologie" for comment.

The aim of the course is to answer the question, "Was ist die klassische Philologie?"[38] The first answer is given, as might be expected, by running through the history of the subject up to the quarrel of Hermann and Böckh (on which only a few remarks, unfortunately). The contribution of Bentley is precisely estimated. Ritschl then moves on to a "Systematischer Theil," which endeavours to show (1) how philology is a unified subject, but (2) maintains an independent position beside other disciplines. Philology will forever be unified and distinguished from mere history by the central position of poetry; but it is distinguished from literary studies by being historically oriented and seeking out the cultural, religious, artistic, and scientific ideals of the past. The course amounts to a clear statement of Ritschl's philological aims, which Gildersleeve elsewhere described as an attempt to mediate between Gottfried Hermann's literary scholarship and Böckh's historical, comprehensive *Altertumswissenschaft*.[39] The notebook unfortunately ends just after the beginning of the second part of the course; similar material is contained, however, in the lectures on criticism and hermeneutics. On the last page of the book we have the interesting remarks:

> Alterthumswissenschaft . . . von Wolf erschaffen; der Name ist zu vieldeutig — Einseitig in Beziehung auf den Gegenstand ist die Philologie gar nicht — nur unbestimmt mit Beziehung auf die Periode.

He objects to the vagueness of the term, although he does not want to restrict philology to any one subject, and holds also that the first part of the term is too exclusive. The inclusion of the afterlife of antiquity as an integral part of the discipline is more characteristically a European perspective than a German one.[40]

Apart from the student notebooks from Germany, one survives from his year at Princeton (1847–1848), entitled "Lectures on Rhetoric and Belles-lettres." Gildersleeve's later opinion of the college in those days was not high,[41] and his diary for the period offers nothing to contradict it (see below). To judge from the notes in this volume the lectures were third-rate. The book includes some miscellaneous scraps — for example, a programme of senior addresses, Nassau Hall, 2nd division, 30 September 1848. Amid such topics as "The Utility of the Classics," "Religious Principle as the Ground of Individual Development," and "False and True Glory," Gildersleeve speaks on "The Poetical Element of the Theory of Preëxistence" (text not preserved).

Other, non-student notebooks (or bundles of notes tacked together) date mostly to the period after 1876. To read, identify, sort, and evaluate the information contained in these books, which number 46 in my list, might seem a bewildering amount of labor. Many of them merely contain abstracts of books, a circumstance that may make the task somewhat easier. But even here the reader must be careful. Gildersleeve habitually made detailed abstracts of books he read,[42] but his résumés were less an abridgement than a re-casting. One is never sure how much is Gildersleeve, how much the original author, so complete is this re-writing and so overpowering the effects of Gildersleeve's style. Many pages of Brief Mention pose the same problem.

Those notebooks not devoted to abstracts contain everything from drafts of articles, letters, speeches, Brief Mention, or lectures, to notes affecting the business of the *American Journal of Philology*; everything from exercises and examination questions to administrative papers, newspaper clippings, and translations from Greek authors.[43] From this farrago I single out a few items for comment.

One notebook contains material for a commentary on Aristophanes' *Frogs*. Unfortunately the comments on individual lines are disappointingly brief; many are radically abbreviated, as "see [my] Pindar" or "discuss syntax." On the other hand there is a series of short, one- or two-paragraph essays on a variety of topics such as "Repetitions in Aristophanes," "Etymology," "Oaths," "Relations with Audience," or "παρὰ προσδοκίαν." His target date for completion, written on the inside front cover, was 1891; what prevented him is a mystery. At *AJP* 37 (1916) 373 (=*Gildersleeve 6*, p. 357), Gildersleeve reports that "for years I worked at an edition of the Frogs that was to have been illustrated by parallels from the annals of literary persiflage." That he felt able to predict a date of completion possibly implies that the date was in sight. The brevity of the notes does not make against this inference; also surviving in part is the first draft of his *Pindar: The Olympian and Pythian Odes* (1885, 1890²), which is in a comparable state. We have the penultimate draft, too; and although it is much farther advanced than these Aristophanic notes, it is still very far from fair copy. Thus the commentary on the *Frogs* need be only two steps from completion, or about fifteen months, if he worked at the same pace as he did for the *Pindar*.[44]

It is possible to be so precise about the time span because everything is dated in the two books of Pindaric notes. The first book is stored in a file labeled by a librarian "Pindaric Studies Nov. 7, 1882–Dec. 28, 1882 and Lectures on Greek Lyric Poetry 1882," which dates are inaccurate, as we shall see in a moment. The book begins with the course of lectures, or more precisely, with an outline of them followed by remarks for incorporation into the first two lectures of the series. Thereafter, and also scattered throughout the book, are what seem to be the first drafts of the commentary for the Olympian odes and the first five *Pythians*.[45] The notes are very scanty, especially for *Olympians* 5, 10(11), and 14. The last note is dated 23 March 1882. On pages 20–38, Gildersleeve has compiled a list of all the figures and tropes in the *Olympians* and in *Pythian* 1.1–20. Page 33 bears the date of 22 April 1876. The whole of this part was presumably composed then, and the notes for the lectures on lyric could date anywhere from 1876 to 1882. The series of 1876 was revised from time to time, as comparison with other notebooks in the collection shows. However, anything in this notebook relating to the Pindaric commentary is securely dated to 1882. On pages 39–45, there is a draft of a lecture on symmetry in Pindar, dated 22 December 1882. A résumé was published in the *J.H.U. Circulars* for August 1883, pages 138–40; the leading ideas reappear throughout the published commentary. From page 97 to the end of the book are written the introductions to the poems, less the notes on the historical background with which these sections regularly begin in the published version, and less the metrical notes with which they end; in other words, the summaries of the poems' contents together with comments on their general form and intent. These summaries are in many ways the most important part of the commentary.[46] They were written at one go between 8 November and 28 December 1882, interrupted only by the essay on symmetry, which of course stated the principles of their composition. The urgency with which Gildersleeve worked may be gathered from the date of 25 December on the introductions to *Pythians* 7 and 8.[47]

The second notebook, "Pindaric Studies Mar. 7–Nov. 5 1882" (librarian's designation), contains notes on *Olympians* 5, 10(11), 14 and all the *Pythians* — that is, for the most part poems either not included or not well represented in the first book. All the notes in this volume are much closer to the final product. They were written between 7 March and 5 November 1882, most of them therefore after the notes in the first book. A timetable in the cover states that the "rough commentary" was completed 7 November; it allows, apparently, for only one more revision, to be done by 1 May. It is possible that for the poems found only in the first book the author proceeded straight from very rough state to fair copy, but it seems fairly certain that an intermediate draft has perished together with the rough draft for the poems found only in the second book.

Also in the second book are notes on the historical background of each poem, for incorporation into the introductions. This was a purely mechanical job and could be done at any time. Inside the covers and on the flyleaves there are drafts of a more extensive preface than the one eventually printed.[48] Also on the back cover is a timetable for the work, as already mentioned. Gildersleeve planned to finish the rough commentary by 1 December, but, he notes later, made it by 7 November; the "critical revision of text" was to be completed by 1 February; "revision of commentary vv. 2213 in 20 weeks — fr[om] Dec. 1 say 1 May 83"; then the "[general] Introduction finished" by 1 July. Of the latter no draft survives. Below the timetable he adds "special job — summary of strophes — begun Nov. 8 — finished after a fashion Dec. 28." On the facing page there is a note: "An independent meditation on the twenty-six odes — Begun Nov. 8 — to be finished in four weeks." It almost seems that these important sections were an afterthought, written because Gildersleeve found himself with three or four weeks of extra time. Nonetheless it remains true that they contain the essence of his approach to Pindar, realizing critical principles passionately declared throughout his career.

The book was not published until 1885, and it is possible that the commentary underwent a further revision after 1 July 1883. But I think that no radical revision occurred; if anything, only a cosmetic one. There may be unknown reasons for the delay; or the truth may be that Gildersleeve did *not* finish the final revision by 1 May, nor the Introductory Essay by 1 July. To judge from the tenses of the verbs in the timetable and the dates of notes in the book itself, Gildersleeve's initial projections were made sometime between March and November 1882. On November 8 or thereabouts he recorded that he had finished the rough commentary and begun the "independent meditation." Around 28 December he records that this was finished. Nothing points to any entry in the book after this date; "Introduction finished July 1 1883" means "to be finished July 1 1883," since it follows directly on the heels of a statement in the future tense, written with the same pen at the same time. If this reconstruction is correct, that the final revision took much longer than expected, the interpretation of an exclamation mark written in pencil beside the date of 1 May 1883 may be that it is a sign of amuse-

ment registered at a later date when he realized that this projection had
been unrealistic. But this is only a guess. For what it is worth we may
note that the summaries took a month longer than expected, being
completed 28 December instead of 1 December, when his period of extra time created by the early completion of the rough draft expired. He
was therefore at least a month late in starting the final revision.

Yet another book contains detailed notes on Pindaric syntax together with statistical tables. On the first four pages is written a remarkable preface showing that Gildersleeve planned to write a book on the
syntax of Pindar.[49] Moreover, this book was to be the first in a series of
syntaxes exploring the language by genre: the next volume was to be a
syntax of the orators, followed by another for the historians; then the
philosophers, comedy, tragedy, and epic. The reasons given for this
wildly ambitious plan amount to one of the earliest and most complete
statements of Gildersleeve's philological ideals, ideals that he main-
tained with absolute consistency for the rest of his life. To summarize
the contents briefly here, Gildersleeve argues that if historical syntax
means the mere chronological registration of phenomena as they appear and disappear in the literature, it is of little value. A language is an
organism; true syntax is biology. It aims to study the inner forces of a
language that account for the life and unity of its outward forms. Time
is not such a force. The real historian inquires into the contribution of
individuals, of races, and, when it comes to literature, of genre. The
ultimate purpose of syntactical studies is an aesthetic one: to lay bare
the splendour of the Greek soul as it is mirrored in the language, and to
appreciate the beauties of the literature.

He proposes to demonstrate the "aesthetic importance of the
study" with the first volume on Pindar. But his normal order in the
classroom was different; he usually began with the orators or the historians, who are here second and third in the list. The rest follow in
proper order; it was a firmly established sequence which Gildersleeve
considered logically and pedagogically sound.[50] Why does he abandon
it here? One reason he gives is that the two "extremes" of syntax, epic
and ordinary speech, meet in Pindar. This sounds weak. A second reason is possibly concealed in an illegible place in the manuscript. But I
suspect the real reason is not that Pindar best illustrates his thesis (he
could prove the thesis with any author); the real reason is that
Gildersleeve loves the poet.

The preface is dated 5 April 1882. About a month earlier
Gildersleeve had begun to write the penultimate draft of his commen-

tary. But he was not yet certain that a commentary was what he wanted to do. He had in fact already devoted considerable labor to the preparation of the syntax, as he says in his preface, and as the notes in this book make clear.[51] A rational exposition of his scholarly aims suggested the syntax. But at some point he threw the scheme over in favor of the book that he called "the only book I ever made as a labor of love."[52] In this connection the remarks in the aborted preface are significant:

> It is an arduous undertaking to make oneself acquainted with the syntactical usage of the classic Greek language from Homer to Menander. Such a task calls for division of labor, and yet it is [at] any rate a more healthful pursuit to follow the game up and down the hills and dales of Greek literature than to sort it when conveniently huddled up in the poulterer's yard. What if a man throws aside his notebook now and then and gives himself up to the pure enjoyment of his authors? He who does not yield to such temptation has not sensitiveness enough to make his observations worth anything.[53]

Throwing aside his notebook seems to be exactly what Gildersleeve did. The world may be grateful for it.

This planned syntax of the departments of Greek literature actually represents a departure from an earlier intention to write a general syntax of classical Greek. Gildersleeve tells us in the preface of the syntax he eventually did write that he had long planned the work, even before his *Latin Grammar* of 1867.[54] A notebook of 1874 survives that seems to represent an expansion of this pre-1867 version. In it are hundreds of examples of conditional clauses, relative clauses, and participles, all neatly organized and outfitted with explanations. A note on page 59 says, "begin here May 24 98," and other notes written with the same pencil and the same slant show him reworking the material yet again, presumably to form part of the *Syntax of Classical Greek*, rather than for some article. This part of the *Syntax*, however, never saw print. The second part was delayed for twelve years owing to the insufferable slowness of his collaborator C. W. E. Miller;[55] and the third part never appeared because of Gildersleeve's own perfectionism. It was to have dealt with the prepositions, and he was unable to convince himself that his definitions were adequately formulated. In fact, as J. A. Scott informs us, the whole project would have been finished long before 1900 (the date of the publication of Part I), were it not for that particular stumbling block.[56] But there were other reasons for the delay. For one thing, the call to Baltimore came in 1876, and the *Journal*, on which

Gildersleeve spent untold hundreds of hours, was established in 1880. Another reason may be provided by our unpublished preface: his basic conception of the task underwent serious modifications. Actually, he tells us in his preface of 1900 that "a catena of syntactical usage would be a memorable achievement, and I do not deny that at one time I thought it possible to organize such a work, for which a large staff of helpers would have been needed; but I have learned to renounce this ambitious scheme."[57] But without the material from the archive we could not have known how much he toyed with this idea or how far he went with it.

The following may be offered as a tentative reconstruction of the history of the *Syntax*. Originally it was to have made a pair with the *Latin Grammar* — a school text. For some reason Gildersleeve was not happy with it and did not publish what he had in 1867. Probably he was, as later, dissatisfied with his formulations. Sometime between 1867 and 1876, when a series of articles began that show a consistently generic orientation, he started to grapple with this concept of historical syntax. Insofar as anything can be concluded from the order of the examples in the 1874 notebook, the importance of genre had not made itself fully felt by that date. By 1882, however, the theoretical apparatus supporting his investigations was completely in place. He seems to be committed to a scheme of monstrous proportions, which no one could have carried out unaided. At this point the other two considerations mentioned above — the lack of time and his perfectionism — asserted or reasserted themselves. Finally, he compromised and produced what he did, which looked far more like the book planned in 1867 than the one dreamed of in 1882, but by the simple expedient of arranging the illustrations of his rules in order of genre he was able to remain more or less faithful to the ideal.

*4. Books and Offprints.* Gildersleeve's books were left to the university, but even if a list were to be found it would probably not be worth the effort of checking them all for marginalia. The few odd books that have somehow been kept separate and stored in Special Collections have no comments of any import. Extensive marginalia will be found only in offprints of some of his own essays, specifically "Problems in Greek Syntax,"[58] "The Legend of Venus,"[59] and "On the Steps of the Bema";[60] rather fewer in this last case. An exception is a copy of W. S. Teuffel's "Übersicht der platonischen Literatur" (Progr. Tübingen 1874), which has some marginalia.

*5. Diaries.* Three diaries survive, together with a fourth book that belongs in the same category. The latter is a "commonplace book" containing a record of the author's readings along with general ruminations from the period January 1848–April 1855. It is carefully indexed by Gildersleeve himself, and a close study would be most revealing for the character of the young man.

The same naturally applies to the three diaries: 1847, 1850–1852, 1852–1853. The first is the record of his time at Jefferson College, Pennsylvania, and Princeton. As he tells us elsewhere, his time was mostly spent in reading literature, since the effort required for his studies was not great.[61] The entry for 23 September sums up his attitude and gives a glimpse of the earnest and conscientious, but by no means dull young man seen everywhere in the book:

> I do not think in future life, I shall expatiate much on the pleasure of college days. I have no taste for liquor, to me the card table presents no allurements, smoking is expensive — and I am far from being mischievous or rowdy. I do not study for honors — and therefore what right have I to be at college? None in the world.

The diary of 1850–1852, though revealing of Gildersleeve's character (especially his literary ambitions), is disappointing if one expects to peer through the windows of a nineteenth century German lecture room for glimpses of the great masters. A fairly close scansion revealed hardly a word about Gildersleeve's academic experiences. Even his beloved Ritschl, whose bust adorned his study in later life,[62] appears only in brief notes like "attended R's lectures." Most entries, if they do not perfunctorily describe a day's routine, deal with nonacademic matters. When the author takes holidays his entries become prolix as he relates every experience at length.

However, there are a few interesting notes near the beginning, when the impressionable young man first arrived in Germany. At his matriculation in Berlin (5 October 1850 — entry for 6 October) he met Böckh, who seemed as desiccated as he was famous:

> He kept us lingering for some time in the antechamber — at the expiration of which definite period my fellow matriculee and myself were ushered into his august[63] presence — A hard featured old cock[64] with lineaments resembling Torrey's[65] but with none of the feisty liveliness which characterized that glorious worthy — The distinguished philologist was exceedingly monosyllabic — asked me my name — told me to hold my matriculation — gave me leave to depart and bowed me out.

A few days later Gildersleeve attended one of his lectures (entry 10 October): "His delivery is abominable and I lost a good deal — which I regret to say troubles me very little." Bekker's intentionally atrocious delivery is described elsewhere by Gildersleeve;[66] here (30 October) he calls it "miserable—almost totally unintelligible." Franz Bopp is "awfully dull" (19 November). But few of us would care to have our performances judged for posterity by a student's diary. A more trustworthy entry confesses (7 October 1850): "If I can succeed this year in making Greek easy and in writing Latin without much difficulty I shall do wonders." His philological grounding was sadly inadequate;[67] the enormous effort required to remedy the situation would have seemed oppressive. In view of the disadvantages with which he started, it is remarkable that he completed his doctorate as quickly as he did.

The diary for 1852–1853 is little different. No comments are passed on his teachers or reports made on the progress of his dissertation. Perhaps the only indication of the intensity with which he must have worked is contained in an entry for 19 May 1852, shortly after his arrival in Bonn: "My life is a *Text-Ausgabe ohne Varianten.*"[68]

*6. Miscellany.* Under this head I include all such oddments as are left: for example, a bundle of photographs of Greek manuscripts, some looseleaf notes on Gildersleeve's ancestry, a shoe-box of cards containing citations from Greek authors, an outline of the programme in the department of philology for 1877, and a picture of J. H. Schmidt as a young man. A few items call for particular comment.

There are two books of memorabilia collected by one S. G. Oliphant,[69] containing apart from copies of some of Gildersleeve's published writings many newspaper clippings of varying degrees of interest. Correspondence between Gildersleeve and Oliphant is also preserved here.

Another book of clippings assembles newspaper reviews of *Hellas and Hesperia* (1909). The extent to which this book was reviewed in the popular press is a sobering indication of Gildersleeve's renown.

There is a notebook belonging to a student, in which some of Gildersleeve's lectures on Greek tragedy are recorded (no date). It is a fair copy, "taken from the original notebook"; consequently it is coherent and clear, although no one would vouch for its accuracy. Still, some glimpses of Gildersleeve in the flesh come through, for example on page 15, where he is quoted as saying that "no man ever raised himself by his own suspenders."

Finally, there is the manuscript of an unpublished novel. Volume I is entitled "Schlafhausen or One Year of Mr. Alfred Thistledown's Life," and dated October 1855; volume II is "Schlafhausen or Confessions of a Very Young Man," February 1856. Before going to Germany,

Gildersleeve had nearly decided to pursue a literary career, and he said on repeated occasions throughout his life that he was a *littérateur manqué*.[70] After returning from Europe (1853), he had to wait three years for a college appointment; indeed, he nearly despaired of getting one. His literary aspirations welled up again, and he had enough time, being employed only in occasional teaching and scholarly writing, to give them play in this novel.[71] Elsewhere Gildersleeve's purely creative writing is poetry. It is also for the most part of an autobiographical cast. Ostensibly, this book is not autobiographical, but it does draw heavily on the author's experiences. The plot has to do with the adventures of a sportive, not to say profligate student in Germany. Gildersleeve was not profligate, of course, but such changes to the central character need be only cosmetic. On the other hand, in an outline on page 63 of the first volume he writes that he has chosen the first person form of narrative for artistic reasons, and begs the public not to identify him with the hero. Still, *qui s'excuse, s'accuse*. I would not pass judgment on the book without closer reading, but we may perhaps be grateful for being spared a work that is *prima facie* immature in conception. Gildersleeve must have had his reasons for suppressing it.

## II. Some Documents of Interest

*1. Gildersleeve and Wilamowitz*. In an important article, W. M. Calder III answered the puzzling question of why these two great men had so little to do with each other.[72] Quite apart from the many opportunities afforded by their work for correspondence, Gildersleeve made at least seven trips to Europe between 1880 and 1905;[73] yet he made no attempt to seek out his celebrated counterpart. The material published by Calder reveals that a devil was at work in the person of Emil Hübner, a fellow student of Gildersleeve's at Bonn and a lifelong friend.[74] Hübner had fallen afoul of Theodor Mommsen, and extended his hatred to include the historian's son-in-law. Because of his slanders, Gildersleeve apparently felt no inclination to make Wilamowitz's acquaintance; for his part the Berlin scholar believed that Gildersleeve hated him.

In 1907 things were put right. Wilamowitz had revealed his ideas about Gildersleeve to Edward Fitch, his only American doctoral student. Although he knew of Gildersleeve's hatred, he said, he could not answer in kind: he acknowledged Gildersleeve's "great services to philology in America," and called him "venerable."[75] Fitch was astonished to learn of Wilamowitz's misapprehension and replied that there must be a

mistake.[76] At the same time he wrote to Gildersleeve, passing on Wilamowitz's compliments but not the rest.[77] Between then and June,
Gildersleeve made a trip to Berlin and decided to call on Wilamowitz.
The two became instant friends, and past misunderstandings were
sorted out.[78] Wilamowitz gave Gildersleeve the grand tour, and even
introduced him "with a certain amount of fanfare" to his students
(about 400!) in the lecture-hall.[79]

Of course, Gildersleeve already knew much about Wilamowitz's
work and character; on the other hand, Wilamowitz knew, apparently,
little of the former and next to nothing of the latter.[80] Accordingly, he
was the one who had the most to gain from the meeting. It is true that as
far as scholarly influence is concerned the situation changed little, although after this Wilamowitz seems to have taken rather more notice of
Gildersleeve's work.[81] But Gildersleeve's personality appealed to him directly, and his existing respect became profound. This is evident from
the brief description of the event in his memoirs, where he again calls
Gildersleeve "venerable,"[82] from the letters published by Calder, and
from the new material published below.

First, a letter from Wilamowitz to Gildersleeve. When he edited
his documents, Professor Calder wrote that no such letter was known to
have survived, although two were attested.[83] This is not one of those
two. The reason its existence at Baltimore was unknown is that it was
stored apart from the correspondence in a file marked "to be catalogued." I found it only because I worked through the whole archive
systematically, without primary reference to the catalogue.

The letter acknowledges receipt of *Hellas and Hesperia*, which was
published 28 August 1909, though not sent before 30 October, when
Gildersleeve wrote to Wilamowitz and promised a copy.[84] However,
even if we allow two or more months for the book to arrive, Wilamowitz
was still unusually slow in writing—he was anything but a "lazy corres-
pondent," as he claims in the first line[85]—and in fact had not read the
whole book even when he did write. It was not for lack of will, as the
letter shows, but for lack of time. Calder writes about his activities this
year:

> It was a difficult year. Wilamowitz was in Copenhagen lecturing 5–9
> March, at a meeting in Rome 2nd week of May. Reading English was a
> chore although easier after his 1908 visit to England. He also (by the way)
> wrote *Staat und Gesellschaft*! . . . in March 1910 the attack of the George
> Circle on Wilamowitz was published (Hellas und Wilamowitz)[86] and that
> must have taken up some time.

The letter also deals with Pindar's seventh *Nemean*. Gildersleeve had sent him an offprint of his piece in the *Journal*,[87] which had been written in direct response to and disagreement with Wilamowitz's own interpretation.[88] Wilamowitz could react unpleasantly to adverse criticism; but large targets attract snipers, and he had a good many to contend with. One can understand that his contempt was occasionally misplaced. No such tone will be found here; rather the opposite, and that to an American. Their disagreement is put down to the complexity of the poet himself rather than to his interpreters' error. That is no polite evasion but the truth of the matter.

Westend-Berlin
1 VII 10
Eichenallee 12

Hochverehrter Herr[89]

ein fauler Briefschreiber[90] und in der beschwerlichsten Arbeitszeit des Sommers möchte ich nicht wieder mir die Sünden auf das Gewissen laden, die es drückt, seit ich Ihr köstliches Hellas and Hesperia empfing, und immer darüber schreiben wollte—was ich nun doch nicht tue. Es liegt noch auf meinem Arbeitstische, und ich greife gern danach, denke auch mit dieser Lektüre manchem Collegen eine Freude zu machen. Sie drücken jeder Äusserung so viel Persönlichkeit auf, und die Eigentümlichkeit des Urteils reizt eben so stark wie der Schliff des Ausdruckes, daß des künstlerischen Genusses fast noch mehr ist als der Belehrung. Das gilt auch von Ihrer Erklärung des pindarischen Gedichtes, stehe sie mit meiner Auffassung in stärkerem oder geringerem Widerspruche. Wir lieben den Dichter—das tun wenige, und seine Sprache ist uns lebendig—das gilt auch für wenigere. Ich wünschte, wir fühlten noch mehr gleich, aber es ist wohl ein Compliment für den Dichter, daß wir es nicht tun. Ich rechne[91] ihn allerdings für einen, der sehr bewusst schafft und einfache Gedanken künstlerisch einkleidet,[92] traue also auf die Erklärung, die dieser Finesse nachgeht. Doch einerlei—ich will jetzt nur danken und Sie meiner aufrichtigen und sehr herzlichen Verehrung versichern: seien Sie darum immer versichert.[93]

UvWilamowitz

Wilamowitz repeated his sentiments some years later in a letter (29 March 1929) to Hermann Collitz[94] acknowledging receipt of the latter's contribution to his eightieth birthday fund. Collitz had mentioned the death of Gildersleeve (1924); Wilamowitz's last sentence is: "Gildersleeves Besuch ist mir noch in lebhafter Erinnerung; er hat mir wirklich imponiert."

For his part Gildersleeve continued in the admiration he had al-

ways had for Wilamowitz. No matter what Hübner had told him, or
what ironical remarks he had printed in the pages of the *Journal*, he
never felt any malice toward Wilamowitz or doubted his worth.[95] Below
is a letter written to his son-in-law, Gardiner M. Lane, son of George
Martin Lane of Harvard, an old friend of Gildersleeve's who had pre-
ceded him to Germany by one year.[96] The Harvard faculty wanted Wilamowitz to come as an exchange professor and had asked Gardiner,
who was a banker but had official connections with the university, to
enlist his father-in-law's help. Gildersleeve felt the trip would be a disas-
ter and would not jeopardize his relations with Wilamowitz by asking
him to come.

The letter exists in three drafts; double square brackets enclose
material from the second draft that was left out of the fair copy. The
amount of re-writing is unusual and shows extra care.

15 Feb. 1911

Dear Gardy:

I hold Professor von Wilamowitz [[who is indisputably the foremost
Greek scholar in the world[97]]] in high esteem and our personal relations
are very pleasant. In fact, I may consider him my friend. And it is just
because of these relations that I should hesitate to approach him on the
subject of coming to Harvard as exchange professor [[if that is what you
mean by asking me to help you]]. Indeed I do not see how I could advise
him to relinquish his wonderful work [[as a writer and lecturer at home]]
for the sake of the classical department at Harvard [[especially as I cannot
say with conviction that it would be as fine a thing for your University as
you think. Most of these great Germans are disappointing when they
come to be embarrassed by an unfamiliar idiom.[98] Much of Wilamowitz's
power resides in his full use of his mother tongue.]] When he lectured at
Oxford[99] he lectured in German. If he attempted English he would certainly fail of producing the effect of which I myself have been witness.
[[the effect he is accustomed to produce on his vast Berlin audiences.[100]]]
So you see I cannot give a hasty answer to your hurried note. I will think
the thing over. Needless to say, if you succeed in getting Wilamowitz, I
shall do my best — as I have done in other cases — to make his sojourn in
America pleasant. [[Of course if you should tempt him to exile himself for
a time and he should do me the honor of consulting me, I shall do what I
can conscientiously to further your cause and I shall assure him of a cor-
dial reception in Baltimore.]][101]

On the other hand, Gildersleeve was not one to prostrate himself.
In fact, he rarely wrote about Wilamowitz, whether before or after their
meeting, without the twinkle of his famous irony dancing about the

edges of his words. The most eloquent of his tributes is accompanied by a teasing reminder of a metrical howler.[102] No such mischievousness is apparent when he is speaking, for example, of Jebb or Henri Weil. The reason for the difference is that Gildersleeve could not resist a tilt at pomposity or pretentiousness, and Wilamowitz was immune to neither. If with his imperfect English Wilamowitz misapprehended the tone of some of the remarks in Brief Mention, it cannot have helped his idea that Gildersleeve hated him. One wonders what he would think to hear himself called "the rough rider of classical philology."[103]

Several unpublished remarks are in keeping with the character of Gildersleeve's published ones. This from one of his lectures on Aristophanes:

> There are doubtless some in my audience whom the name Κυδαθηναιεύς will stir like the sound of a trumpet and call up the pugnacious German scholar Wilamowitz-Möllendorff and his raids into every nook and corner of philological territory. . . .[104]

From another lecture on Aristophanes:

> Against this tradition [of Megarian comedy] Ulrich von Wilamowitz-Moellendorff has resolutely set his face[105] a brilliant scholar to whom a face has been given chiefly for the purpose of setting it against everything, and so we must expect him now and again to flatten his nose against the most transparent pane in the casement of the Palace of Truth. He is delightful reading, is Udalricus de Wilamowitz-Moellendorff, whether he is right or wrong. He writes Latin elegiacs with a portentous hiatus in the wame of the pentameter[106] and composes truly German versions of Greek tragedies,[107] but he is a good scholar for all that and a most surprising genius, like his War Lord William the Sudden. . . .[108]

Although it deals with German scholarship in general rather than Wilamowitz particularly, I cite here this passage from yet another lecture on Aristophanes—vintage Gildersleeve:

> [The Germans] have done a great deal of harm in taking everything in the most serious way. If a Scotchman's hard skull has to be trepanned in order to let in a joke, the German brain, with its immense vaporizing power, makes out of the simplest dew drop a mist that swamps the universe, and the Dread Earnestness of Fun is a spectre that haunts all their historical works. They have made a Preacher of Righteousness out of Aristophanes, a manner of John the Baptist out of the joyous old Baldhead, and have evolved the deepest political maxims out of his most trivial jests.[109]

A few incidental remarks may be reported from Gildersleeve's correspondence with H. L. Ebeling, who obtained his doctorate from the Johns Hopkins University in 1892 and went on to a long teaching career at Goucher College. In a letter of 15 April 1906, Ebeling had expressed disbelief at what seemed to be a crude error in one of Wilamowitz's works and was hesitant to call it such in print. Gildersleeve replies on the twenty-first: "You need not be afraid of Wilamowitz. He makes all manner of rash statements and takes them back with a joyousness that disarms criticism." On 8 May he replies to another letter: "Like many good people (Polybius) bores me and I can't judge him calmly. Wilamowitz's opinion of him does not move me, because as you intimate he loves to turn the world upside down."[110] On 22 September 1907 Ebeling wrote to say that he had missed Gildersleeve on a trip to Baltimore and would have enjoyed hearing about the meeting with Wilamowitz. He had heard of it from Fitch; in fact he had probably seen the letter from Wilamowitz, since he refers to the latter's pleasure at Gildersleeve's "mental vigor and freshness," or "geistige Rüstigkeit und Frische," as the original has it.[111] Gildersleeve replies on the twenty-fifth:

> It would have been a pleasure to talk over my trip with you. But the philological part of it was limited to my interviews with Wilamowitz and Vahlen and the impressions were so deep that they are not likely to be softened[112] before we meet again.

A fitting conclusion to this section may be provided by some remarks in a letter of Gildersleeve to Kirby Flower Smith of 7 August 1910, found in the archive by Professor Briggs:

> I have received the half-dreaded letter from Wilamowitz about the Seventh Nemean. I do not undertake to read between the lines. It was a hard letter for him to write, but it is generous and kindly. Perhaps "considerate" is the best word. One bears with an ancient creature like myself, thinking that it will not be for long. But I have developed a toughness that is a surprise to me and indulgence may be misplaced.

Briggs comments appropriately (*per litteras*): "Certainly an extreme of *Selbstironie* to think that Wilamowitz-Moellendorff was kind to him only *antiquitatis causa*."

  2. *Gildersleeve and Vahlen.* The respectful reference made above to Johannes Vahlen[113] finds parallels in several places of the *Journal*.[114] The two men became acquainted in their student days at Bonn, where Vahlen was a regular member of Ritschl's seminar and Gildersleeve was a *Zuhörer*.[115] The esteem Gildersleeve developed at that time was main-

tained throughout his life. Personal contact, however, does not seem to have been made again until 1907.[116]

There were certain similarities in their scholarship. For both, the cornerstone was the exact observation of linguistic usage. True pupils of Ritschl, they brought an encyclopaedic knowledge to bear on the interpretation of literary texts; both sought to restore the spirit of lost life. When they started out, their scholarship was progressive. It is a matter of history that new movements eclipsed theirs, and Vahlen in particular seems fated to be remembered less for his many brilliant accomplishments than as the redoubtable defender of the "old school" against the onslaught of the Wilamowitzians. That this letter should be written in Latin seems thoroughly fitting.

It acknowledges receipt of the third edition of Gildersleeve's *Latin Grammar* (1894), in which Gonzalez Lodge collaborated. Vahlen at least knows of and has read the other editions; to Usener (next section) the book was new. Gildersleeve was known in Europe — insofar as he was known at all — chiefly as a syntactician.[117] But the *Latin Grammar* (especially in its first two editions of 1867 and 1872) is hardly the touchstone of Gildersleeve's overseas fame, it being an unpretentious schoolbook; Usener's ignorance is no insult, Vahlen's knowledge probably the result of complimentary copies.[118]

The letter was found in the same file "to be catalogued" that contained the letter from Wilamowitz.

B. L. Gildersleevio
S.P.D.
I. Vahlen

Iussi, ut opinor, a Te, Vir clarissime, Tui editores nuper ad me miserunt with compliments of the Authors grammaticae Latinae Gildersleevianae tertium iam editae exemplar. Pro qua re, quam-quam et illis, sicuti par est, gratiam habeo, agere tamen gratias Tibi malui auctori Tuoque laboris socio, quod me non indignum habuistis, cui opus Tuum iam pridem celebratum mittendum curaretis. Perlegi igitur non totam grammaticam sed partes quasdam selectas, velut caput illud locupletissimum, cui Formation of Words inscriptum est, et alterum, quo de compositarum sententiarum generibus agitur, hoc est capita ea quae vulgo in grammaticis nostris non ita tractari solent; sed facile mihi persuasi, in his quidem partibus quas cognovi rationes vos iniisse perquam probabiles librumque Tuum sive Vestrum, si quid indicare possum, perutilem fore et ad studiorum usum egregie accommodatum.

Vale mihique favere perge.
Berolini, d. III. m. Ianuari
    a. MDCCCXCV

*3. Gildersleeve and Usener.* Gildersleeve's warm tribute to Hermann Usener (1834–1905) upon his death is but one of the places where he records his feelings for this wonderful scholar.[119] They first met in 1880 and renewed their contact many times thereafter, often by letter, once personally in 1888.

Their correspondence is partially preserved in two places: eight letters from Gildersleeve among Usener's papers in the Universitätsbibliothek, Bonn; and two letters from Usener together with a draft of one from Gildersleeve in the lucrative "to be catalogued" file. The fair copy of the latter is one of the eight in Bonn, and it is that copy which is printed below along with Usener's two letters from the Baltimore archive.

Of especial importance is the paragraph in the first letter in which Usener discusses his *Götternamen*, soon to be published. Usener's work on religion has largely been superseded, either by advancing research on particular problems or by the development of new approaches. Nonetheless, one still has to consult him on many occasions. Certainly his position in the history of the discipline is secure as one of the first of those in Germany who attempted in the wake of Mannhardt to understand not merely the mythology of paganism but also its rituals;[120] to penetrate the pagan mind and understand its attitude to the world as a genuine form of religious experience. Not without justice did Dieterich apply the term ἥρως κτίστης.[121]

Usener's influence through his pupils at Bonn, where with Bücheler he brought the "Bonn School" to the peak of its renown, is yet another part of his legacy. The man who can claim to be Hermann Diels' mentor needs no other laurels. Moreover, there are his many writings outside the field of religion, notably the *Epicurea* (1887) and the edition of the *Opuscula* of Dionysius of Halicarnassus (vol. I, 1899), completed by Ludwig Radermacher (vol. II, 1904, 1929[2]). His interests were manifold, yet united by a common purpose best stated by Usener himself in a truly magnanimous letter to the young Wilamowitz: "Sie suchen die Schöpfungen des Willens in der Geschichte, ich das unwillkürliche, unbewußte Werden."[122]

*a. Usener to Gildersleeve.*

Bonn, 15 Nov. 94

Sehr verehrter freund,
    Ihre verlagshandlung in New York hat mir heute die grosse freude gemacht, mir einen zwar indirecten aber sehr inhaltreichen (ich möchte

sagen: saftigen) gruss von Ihnen in gestalt Ihrer bisher mir unbekannt[123] gebliebenen Latin grammar von 1894 zu senden. Ich habe das schöne buch mit begierde angelesen und angeblättert, und will den tag nicht beschliessen ohne Ihnen meinen herzlichen dank für diesen neuen beweis Ihres freundlichen gedenkens auszusprechen. Mir scheint, Sie haben es meisterlich verstanden, die beiden streitenden interessen der praxis und der theorie auszugleichen, und den ergebnissen der wissenschaft in dem schulbuche das wort zu geben. Unsere üblichen schulbücher könnten viel von Ihnen lernen; allmählich werden sie es auch wohl thun, aber es braucht zeit dazu in dem altersmüden Europa.

Wie lange ist es her, dass wir von Ihnen keine directen nachrichten erhalten haben, nach denen wir uns sehnen? Zwar dass Sie die alte rüstigkeit sich bewahren, zeigen ausser diesem buche die in nie stockender reihe sich folgenden hefte Ihres American journal. Aber wie geht es Ihrer frau gemahlin, Ihrer fräulein tochter und dem sohne? Darüber lassen Sie uns gelegentlich doch etwas hören.

Ich bin inzwischen ein "sexagenarius de ponte" geworden, und arbeite mich müde an einem werke,[124] das unter der presse sich befindet, auch einer art grammatik, nur von einer sehr wenig erforschten sprache, der sprache der religion. Von einer art *scienza nuova*, die ich zu gründen versuche, stosse ich den ersten abschnitt ab,[125] weil ich innerlich mit ihm fertig bin und das gefühlt habe, nicht wesentlich weiter zu kommen. Die wissenschaft nenne ich: formenlehre der religiösen vorstellungen, und dieser erste abschnitt soll handeln von der religiösen begriffsbildung (die wir natürlich an den namen der götter zu beobachten haben). Nun können Sie auch wissen, warum ich mich viel mit legenden beschäftige; ich verfolge religiöses denken und träumen, wo ich es finde.

Den meinigen allen geht es wohl. Meine frau ist heute für einige zeit nach Berlin abgedampft, wo seit herbst unser lieblingssohn, der zweite, namens Walter unter Diels philologie studiert. Der älteste ist mit dem abschluss seiner studien (physik) beschäftigt,[126] der jüngste geht dem maturitätsexamen entgegen.

So viel für heute. Mit den herzlichsten grüssen von haus zu haus
Ihr dankbar ergebener
H. Usener
(NS) Grüssen Sie bestens auch herrn Warren[127] und frau von uns.

*b. Usener to Gildersleeve.*

Bonn 23/1, 1901

Sehr verehrter freund und college,
Gestern kam mir durch die freundliche vermittelung der verlagsbuchhandlung der erste theil Ihrer Syntax of classical Greek zu. Schon

die durchmusterung der ersten abschnitte hat mich davon Überzeugt, in
wie selbständiger weise Sie die grosse aufgabe anzugreifen und fördernd
zu behandeln verstanden haben. Ich bin glücklich vor allem Ihretwegen,
dass es Ihnen gelungen ist Ihr lebenswerk zu einem solchen abschlusse zu
führen, und spreche Ihnen dazu mit der vollen empfindung eines war-
men freunds meine glückwünsche aus. Dann aber auch um der sache
willen. Es ist bewundernswerth, mit welcher umsicht Sie eine so reiche
Übersicht des sprachgebrauchs von Homer bis Platon, von dem redneri-
schen kanon ausgehend, aufgestellt, und mit welcher erschöpfenden ge-
nauigkeit und knappen beschränkung Sie dieselbe gegeben haben. Besonders freue ich mich, eine fülle von spracherscheinungen, an denen
sonst der fachmässige grammatiker, weil er nach überkommenem leisten
zu arbeiten liebt, vorbeizugehen pflegt, nun in das syntaktische system
einbezogen zu sehn. Ich schreibe Ihnen unter dem frischen eindruck der
ersten 22 seiten, um nicht in einer zeit starker arbeitsbedrängniss meinen
dank vielleicht länger als mir lieb verschieben zu müssen. Aber ich freue
mich auf alles weitere, das ich schrittweise durchkosten werde. An gele-
gentlichem dissensus wird es nicht fehlen, aber der wird am ersten an
punkten herantreten, die auf Ihren neu eroberten gebieten liegen (wie
z.b. §32-35).[128] Wenn mir irgend zeit dafür verbleibt, wird es mir eine
freude sein, durch eine anzeige unsere landsleute auf Ihr werk hinzu-
weisen. Ich schreibe gleichzeitig an die redaction der Goettinger Gel(ehr-
ten) Anzeigen, um mir diese zeitschrift dafür offen zu halten.[129]

Wollen Sie mir doch gelegentlich sagen, ob unser verleger,
Sauerländer in Frankfurt, meinen auftrag richtig ausgeführt hat, Ihnen
vom Rheinischen Museum (von Band LIV an) ein exemplar gratis zu
übersenden. Weil ich das glaubte voraussetzen zu dürfen, habe ich Ihnen
von den letzten aufsätzen, die ich darin habe erscheinen lassen, keinen
sonderabzug übersandt. Sollte mein auftrag seit 1898/9 vernachlässigt
worden sein, so würde ich sorge tragen, dass Ihnen jene bände nachge-
liefert werden.

Ich bin durch meine augen auf eine sehr kurze, im winter vollends
dürftige arbeitszeit beschränkt.[130] Soweit andere pflichten mir musse offen lassen, beschäftige ich mich eben einmal wieder mit evange-
lienkritik.[131]

Mit den herzlichsten grüssen von haus zu haus
Ihr treu ergebener
H. Usener

NS Ich weiss nicht, ob ich Ihnen seiner zeit mitgetheilt habe, dass unsere tochter Marie sich inzwischen (März 1899) mit prof. Albr(echt)
Dieterich[132] in Giessen (dem Verfasser des Abraxas, der Nekyia,
Pulcinella u.a.) verheirathet hat. Er ist mir ein besonders nahe stehender
früherer schüler, der so ganz in mein religionsgeschichtliches fahrwasser
eingelenkt hat. So können Sie denken, wie glücklich mich diese verbin-

dung gemacht hat. Was macht Ihre liebenswürdige tochter? Und die gat-
tin, die πότνια, der ich mich zu füssen zu legen bitte? und die herrn
söhne?[133]

Nochmals Ihr H.Us.

*c. Gildersleeve to Usener (reply to b.)*[134]

Baltimore 12/II 1901

Verehrtester Freund und College:
Wenn ich in Ihrer schönen Heimath wäre, würde ich gewiss
Deutsch mit Ihnen sprechen. Also sei es gewagt, meinen Dank für den
schönen Brief vom 22. [sic] v.M. auf Deutsch zu sagen. Holperig aber
herzlich.
Möge sich der günstige Eindruck, den die ersten Seiten der Syntax
auf Sie gemacht haben, beim Weiterlesen bestätigen. Aber so viel mir
auch an Ihrem wissenschaftlichen Urteil gelegen ist, kann ich mich doch
im schlimmsten Falle mit dem Zeugnis Ihres unveränderten Wohlwollens
trösten.
Seit einigen Jahren kommt mir das Rheinische Museum regelmäss-
ig zu, aber erst durch Ihren Brief hab' ich erfahren, dass ich die Sendung
Ihrem gütigen Auftrage schulde.[135] Alles, was von Ihrer Feder herrührt,
lese ich, wie Sie wissen, mit tiefstem Interesse und aufrichtiger Bewun-
derung, und es macht mir eine besondere Freude, Ihren Forschungen
nachzugehen, und wenn meine vielfachen Geschäfte es erlauben, dem
amerikanischen Publikum einen Bericht über Ihre Arbeiten zu erstatten.
Meine herzlichen Glückwünsche zu dem schönen Bunde mit dem
geistreichen und geistesverwandten Gelehrten, dessen Nekyia mich höch-
lich interessiert hat.[136]
Dem Gildersleeveschen Hause geht augenblicklich alles gut. Meine
Tochter, die sich vor drei Jahren mit einem Bostoner Bankier Herrn
Lane, dem Sohne eines alten Freundes und Collegen,[137] vermählt hat, ist
die glückliche Mutter eines allerliebsten zweijährigen Mädchens, die mir
*l'art d'être grandpère* sehr leicht gemacht hat, und mein Sohn hat sich zu
einer achtbaren Stellung in New York als Architekt durchgearbeitet.[138]
Meiner Frau hat das verflossene Jahrzehnt wenig angehabt und ich selber
bin noch rüstig und munter, trotz der 70 Jahre. Wir denken oft an die
Bonner Tage und all' die Güte, die Sie und Ihre reizende Gemahlin uns
haben angedeihen lassen.
Meine Frau lässt herzlich grüssen und obgleich sie meine Sehnsucht
nach dem zweiten Bande des Dionysius[139] nicht teilen kann, teilt sie doch
in vollem Masse alle Wünsche für das Wohlergehen Ihres Hauses.
Ihr treu ergebener
B. L. Gildersleeve
Herrn Geheimrath Usener

*4. Gildersleeve and Pindar.* Published here is a preface to an un-finished syntax of Pindar, on the significance of which something has already been said. A more revealing document could scarcely be found; at the same time it is only a draft, written in a discursive, not to say disjointed manner. There are several points at which interpretation is not entirely certain. It is best to print it first and discuss problems second.

Years ago when I came to "a realizing sense," as the preachers say, how hard it was to keep up any truly philological work under the conditions of American life, I determined that while I tried to appreciate every side of the great department which had been assigned to me, I should make the syntax of the Greek language the especial field of my researches. The genesis of forms cannot be explored without a knowledge of comparative grammar and comparative grammar involves Sanskrit, involves phonetics. Textual criticism ought to have grammar and logic—which are not identical—to control it but palaeographical vision is of prime importance and this was denied me. The prosecution of historical research, the solution of literary problems, all that pertains to higher criticism, as it is called, seems to be impossible without a large apparatus.[140] One is forever doing over work that has already been done. And yet it is absolutely necessary to do some individual work, if one is not to degenerate into a mere adapter of other people's results, if one is to have any ground of one's own to stand on. It seemed to me that in the many mansions of Hellenism there were rooms enough that had not yet been explored, measurements not yet taken, cobwebs not yet brushed down, windows not yet opened. I had studied in my early days my Krüger[141] with intense interest and let me hope some profit and like most novices I was very desirous of introducing my favourite grammarian to the English speaking public. The plan never got beyond the stage of a plan, and so several of my projects remained in the first draught. Meantime the work of teaching went on and I was confronted every week with practical problems in Greek composition, which had to be solved provisionally or otherwise.[142] Grammars often failed me. Points clear to my feeling, had to be made clear to my understanding and to the understanding of my classes for I can truly say that I have never been satisfied with any formula, that did not commend itself after one explanation to the sense of my pupils. I began to get sharper views and better rules as it seemed to me than some of those presented in the ordinary text books and though it often happened that I found my discovery to be no discovery and my formula an old recipe, I had the comfort of confirmation. I had thought the thoughts of better grammarians. I renounced for want of time as well as means the study of monographs on special usages and special authors. Numerous when I began they are endless now, and to be candid not very satisfactory. Most of them are written by very young men who have no wide acquaintance with the language, who find mare's nests at every turn, and the best of these dissertations are mere systematized illustrations of the theories of certain grammarians. The more objective they are, the better they are as material for the constructive scholar but then they can hardly be honored with the appellation of intellectual work. It is an arduous undertaking to make oneself acquainted with the syntactical usage of the classic Greek language from Homer to Menander. Such a task calls for division of labor, and yet it is [at] any rate a more healthful pursuit to follow the game up and down the hills and dales of Greek literature than to sort it when conveniently huddled up in the poulterer's yard. What if a man throws aside his notebook now and then and gives himself up to the pure enjoyment of his authors? He who does not yield to such temptation has not sensitiveness enough to make his observations worth anything.

Greek prose composition forced me to look for sharp and clear rules, not to say principles; the interpretation of the earlier monuments of Greek literature forced me to the historical study of the syntax. When I taught Homer, I pointed out the practical differences from Attic, and those practical differences demand and suggest theories of growth, theories of coalescence, of effacement. In the use of the article, of the moods, of the tenses, of the cases, even without the light of comparative grammar we can see the hardening of the plastic expression, the fixing of group,[143] the elimination of needless forms, the bifurcation of constructions. When we pass from Attic prose to Homer we pass from a sphere where *logical grammar* does not seem absurd because the people who used the language had begun to reason about it and think in clear formulae, into a sphere where we are much nearer the *Wendelust* of the earliest time though still at a wide remove from that unattainable presence. I know that *logic* is not a popular word in philology now and that the definition of grammar as applied logic would not find favor among professed students of the growth of language, and yet logic within certain limitations is perfectly justifiable as a grammatical organon in the reflective period of speech. Many of the set phrases of a[144] crystallized language are logical successes. We have a right in Attic to organize our sentences according to metaphysical categories. It is not nonsense to speak of conditional sentences, final sentences, consecutive sentences and the rest, although we are in great danger of talking nonsense, if we transfer these categories as unyielding entities to the older speech. There is in the classic prose of the reflective period very little [that] cannot be put into logical constructions. The only trouble is with fossilized phrases, which can only be explained as fossils are to be explained by going back to a prior life. From the basis of the everyday prose then we work our way up towards the origins. We count backward; we begin to chronologize. This is not history, but this is essential to history. We note the disappearance of certain prose forms as we go back. New constellations rise on our vision. Emergence and disappearance mark our track, sometimes suggestive, sometimes riddlesome. The disappearances we can understand. They are all in the direction of simpli[fi]cation. The emergences are more puzzling. Are they individual, are they dialectic? Does the individual set the pattern, which the people follow; or is a phrase brought up out of the lower stratum of the population by some bold poet or writer? Then we find in a literature with departments so sharply marked as the Greek that the department has its rights—originally dialectic but afterwards artistic, aesthetic, what you will. And so you have another element to deal with. Of course the historical study takes in all these elements, and more. It goes back to the Indo-Germanic parent speech and seeks the common source. But it does not attempt to know too much. If function and form corresponded perfectly, there would be no syntax to learn. The original function, if it can be ascertained, would doubtless enable us better to understand the transformations of use. But this is not so much history as biology, and this biology of a language is an impossibility, because there is no embryology possible. For as the consciousness of the people who speak the language must in many cases be a finality, when the organism is dead to them, it is dead to us, except in phrase survivals.

A syntax of Attic prose may well deal in sharp, clear "rules." There is a growth discernible in it, there is room for individuality in it, but we can calculate on it. A syntax of Homeric poetry brings us face to face with numberless genetic problems. Individuality is at a minimum. We have a host of survivals from the preliterary period, if we are not in the preliterary period itself. We have all the material we shall want. Attic prose is essentially a precipitate from this solution.

In Lyric Poetry, we find a syntax that is very different from Attic prose. It resembles that of the Epos in some respects, and yet it lacks its variety. It is a selection of the epic thesaurus, with especial reference to the requirements of the department. Extremes meet, and in many points the language of the people and the language of higher lyric must have been identical.

If I can succeed in showing the character of this departmental syntax and so vindicating the aesthetic[145] importance of the study, I shall have prepared the way for the other sections of the work, on which I have spent much thought and no little labor. If I should be permitted to complete the task, I shall put in the foreground an oratorical syntax, historically arranged. The historical writers will follow; then the philosophers; Attic comedy, not parodic; Attic tragedy; and then Epic. I recognize lyric as . . . . . . . . . . ,[146] and as I shall have given a full treatment of it in this volume I can make my treatment of it brief.

Such is the scheme of the work, for which I have collected much material. Whether I shall have the courage to carry it out in all its formidable details will depend somewhat on the success of this forerunner. But whatever acceptance my theories may find, I know the philological public too well to hope [for] any mercy for any thought [of] an exhaustive treatment, and I have done my best to make the present volume ////// treatment [a] repertory of facts for Pindaric syntactical usage, with illustrations from the other lyrists, and a conspectus of tragic choral usage. April 5, 1882

He begins by stating why he chose syntax as his area of specialization. The reason given here is a purely practical one: there was not the apparatus in America to support anything else. But as we shall see, there were more compelling reasons than that.

Gildersleeve next informs us that, while plans to introduce the American public to his favorite German grammarian lay in abeyance, the daily pressure of teaching forced him to fashion rules less philological and more suited to the students' needs than Krüger's were. In a digression here he denigrates typically German *Programme*, dissertations, and specialist monographs.[147] More difficult it may be, but more "healthful" to inspect syntactical phenomena in their original setting, in the authors.

Teaching involved him further in the study of historical syntax and the whole question of what historical syntax is ("theories of growth"). At this point his sequence of thought becomes less easy to follow. We notice the differences between Homer and Attic prose, he says; the latter shows a closer relationship of grammar to logic. This thought appears to send him off on a digression on the mutual dependence of these two categories, but the real point of these remarks is to argue that Attic syntax is the τέλος of Greek, its ultimate and perfect state, and that the student should begin with it and work backward ("from the basis of the everyday prose . . . we count backward"). This is a principle that Gildersleeve consistently followed in his teaching.[148]

This moving backward, he says further, leads us to note the disappearance and emergence of various phenomena. We could assemble all such data on a chart; but to do only that would be to write chronology, not history ("we begin to chronologize . . ."). We need causal explanations for the gains and losses of a language; these will be found by inquiring, for example, into the importance of the individual, of the dialect, and, in literature, of the "department" or genre. These and other questions asked, the researcher has begun to write proper history.[149]

There is, however, a certain limit to our knowledge ("it does not attempt to know too much"). The prehistoric state of the language is lost to us because it was already lost to the ancients. Successive states of a language are complete unto themselves.[150] The inner consciousness of the speakers is like the unseen life-force that animates an organism. We cannot study the "biology" of the prehistoric language once this consciousness is lost to subsequent generations; we must have sufficient contemporary material.[151] In more modern terminology, we may have examples of *la parole*, but we cannot recover *la langue*. I take it that Gildersleeve's "function" corresponds exactly to the latter, his "form" and "use" to the former.

For Attic prose and other departments, however, the situation is different. In a few brief words he outlines the salient features of Attic, Homeric, and lyric syntax, *qua* generic syntaxes. In Attic, we can have more certain "rules" than we can for epic. His quotation marks around the word "rules" and the general thought of the sentence can be related to the statement that "if function (*langue*) and form (*parole*) corresponded perfectly, there would be no syntax to learn," and each statement used to explain the other. Syntax exists neither in the realm of supposedly perfect, unchanging *langue*, nor in the realm of uncontrolled, unpredictable, but living *parole*. It involves both. Gildersleeve is stating in an oblique way the paradox that a language, while having rules and correct grammar, is constantly re-fashioned by popular, even uneducated usage.

Finally, he moves on to the purpose of the study, and its place in the projected series. Why is he starting with Pindar? The illegibility of one or more crucial words prevents a certain answer; however, I have already suggested that the real reason is not explicit: it is his love of the poet. Note the expression, "vindicating the aesthetic importance of the study"; the ultimate purpose of grammar was always for Gildersleeve an aesthetic one, viz. the appreciation of the beauty of the Greek language and the sublime spirit expressed by it.[152] The vision of beauty is what motivated Gildersleeve in his syntactical investigations, not merely the practical consideration of a lack of books.

This view of the purpose of Greek studies derives not from German scientific historicism, which Gildersleeve greatly admired, but from English humanism, which shaped the ideals of American education.[153] The highest value of classical Greek lay in its inspiration as a thing of timeless beauty, a model valid for all subsequent ages.[154] Related to this view is another very un-German notion, partially latent in this preface, but explicit in one of his unpublished lectures on Aristophanes.[155] It is that the collection of great masses of details for their own sake is useless.

There is no point in minute investigation without regard to the larger purpose of one's activities. The splendour of the Greek spirit is our final object, and it cannot be studied anywhere except in the different, self-contained phases of a language, each more or less perfect unto itself. We seek the inner "function" of the Attic dialect. Each author gives us his own version of it; Gildersleeve was too good a scholar to think that any one author such as Lysias gives the "best" Attic.[156] Significantly, however, he never devoted any serious attention to inscriptions. The reason was not laziness or ignorance;[157] it was that Atticism was for him not an object to be described as an exercise in historical positivism, but one to be studied in the spirit of cultivated classicism.

Finally I must put in the text, as opposed to the notes, a passage that may be regarded as an abstract of our unpublished preface; or, if you like, the preface may now supply the commentary for a passage whose full meaning could not have been perceived:

> My first interest in Greek Syntax after I had passed the béjaune stage was practical, as I have set forth elsewhere. I tried to get a better formulation of the phenomena for the sake of my classes, and fancied that I had succeeded here and there. Then there came, not all at once, the conviction of the importance of syntax for the appreciation of the various ranges of literature and the art of the individual. Finally all this formulation, all this classification, all this road-making, so to speak, seemed to bring me to the point where I could hope to gain some insight into the way in which the Greek spirit strove to work out the problems of architectural speech— historical syntax in the true sense of the word, not what passes for such, not the mechanical registry of the phenomena as they emerge in literature. The history of Greek syntax is the history of the soul of the Greek people.

These remarks are from the introduction to the "Indiculus Syntacticus," *AJP* 37 (1916) 481. The gap between our preface and these sentences is 34 years; but since we have traced these ideas at least as far back as 1876, we may round the number up to 40. By a happy coincidence Gildersleeve reached his mature conception of scholarship at the same time that he was beginning his momentous career in Baltimore. In all the years he spent there, as the passage quoted above and numerous others in our footnotes show, not one word of his creed changed. It was a simple, clear, and powerful conception, one that combined the best of the English and German traditions as they existed in Gildersleeve's formative years.

I add that qualification advisedly. One ought to bear in mind that

by the time Wilamowitz's conception of philology was beginning to
make itself felt, Gildersleeve was approaching what would now be called
retirement age. It requires an effort of imagination on our part to enter
the pre-Wilamowitz era of classical scholarship; we do not realize how
many of our methods and assumptions, which we regard as self-evident,
are really owed to him. In this light Gildersleeve's achievement is even
more remarkable: the breadth of his knowledge, the depth of his learning, the penetration of his vision.

# NOTES

        Acknowledgments are due and freely given to the Special Collections Division,
Milton S. Eisenhower Library, Johns Hopkins University, for permission to publish and
quote from documents in their possession; to the Handschriftenabteilung, Universitätsbibliothek, Bonn, for permission to publish the letter of Gildersleeve to Usener and to
quote from others in Usener's Nachlaß; to Dr. W. Mommsen, for permission to publish
the letter of Wilamowitz and quote from another (p. 77); to Dr. H. Dieterich, for permission to publish the letters of Hermann Usener; to the Manuscripts Department, Edwin A.
Alderman Library, University of Virginia, for permission to quote from the Gildersleeve
Papers (#4711), note 34 below; to the South Caroliniana Library, University of South
Carolina, for permission to quote from the Yates Snowden Papers, note 116 below; and
principally to Mrs. Katherine Weems, literary heir of Gildersleeve, for permission to
publish all the Gildersleeve documents found here.
        I should like to express publicly my appreciation of the kind reception and assis-
tance accorded by Mrs. A. S. Gwyn and the staff of the Special Collections Division, and
to record the hospitality of the Classics Department of the Johns Hopkins University. In
addition I must mention the scholarly assistance rendered at various stages by E. C.
Kopff, H. Herter, H. J. Mette, and W. Mommsen; by Mr. T. Hofmeister of Johns
Hopkins University; and by my colleagues M. Richter and G. Brude-Firnau. Especially
to be singled out are Professors Ward W. Briggs, Jr. of the University of South Carolina,
and William M. Calder III, of the University of Colorado, who have unselfishly offered
their help at every turn and improved the work throughout.
        [1]In addition to the abbreviations listed at the beginning of this volume, the follow-
ing abbreviations are used: "University Work in America and Classical Philology," presidential address to the American Philological Association, 11 July 1878, printed in the
Princeton Review 55 (1879) 511-36, reprinted with small corrections and some notes in
Gildersleeve 2, 87-123; "Classics and Colleges," Princeton Review 54 (1878) 67-95
(=Gildersleeve 2, 43-84); "Grammar and Aesthetics," Princeton Review 59 (1883) 290-
319 (=Gildersleeve 2, 127-57) (this and the preceding two articles will be quoted from
Gildersleeve 2); "Formative Influences," The Forum 10 (1891) 607-17; "Professorial
Types," The Hopkinsian 1 (1893) 11-18; "Classical Studies in America," Atlantic
Monthly 78 (1896) 728-37; "Oscillations and Nutations of Philological Studies," address
at the Philological Congress, Philadelphia, 27 December 1900, printed in Johns Hopkins
University Circulars 20, no. 151 (1901) 45-50; "A Novice of 1850," Johns Hopkins
Alumni Magazine 1 (1912) 3-9. Note also J.H.U. = Johns Hopkins University; Wilamo-
witz, Erinnerungen = U. von Wilamowitz-Moellendorff, Erinnerungen 1848-1914[2]

(Leipzig 1929); Wilamowitz, *Selected Correspondence* = U. von Wilamowitz-Moellendorff, *Selected Correspondence 1869–1931*, W. M. Calder III, ed., *Antiqua* 23 (Naples 1983); Calder, *Studies* = W. M. Calder III, *Studies in the Modern History of Classical Scholarship, Antiqua* 27 (Naples 1984); *Bonner Gelehrte* = *150 Jahre. Rheinische Friedrich-Wilhelms-Universität zu Bonn 1818–1968. Bonner Gelehrte. Beiträge zur Geschichte der Wissenschaften in Bonn. 5. Philosophie und Altertumswissenschaften* (Bonn 1968).

[2]The reform of higher education in America began earlier with the foundation of Cornell (1868) and the reforms at Harvard under Charles W. Eliot (president from 1869), although it may be noted that Johns Hopkins University was already incorporated in 1867. In any event, the German model was most realized in Baltimore. See in general R. L. Church and M. W. Sedlak, *Education in the United States* (New York 1976) 227 f.; R. F. Butts and L. A. Cremin, *A History of Education in American Culture* (New York 1953) 392 f.; S. G. Noble, *A History of American Education* (New York 1954; reprint, 1970) 309.

[3]See Gildersleeve's obituary, *J.H.U. Circulars* n.s. 10 (Dec. 1908) 32–37.

[4]B. L. Gildersleeve, "The Greek Seminary," *J.H.U. Circulars* (June 1910) 3; *Gildersleeve 2*, 499. The physicist H. T. Rowland was hired before him, as an instructor; and Gilman had actually offered the Greek chair first to W. W. Goodwin, who declined and stayed at Harvard: K. A. Jacob, "The Hopkins Four," *Johns Hopkins Magazine* (July 1974), 18 f. See in this volume, Benario, pp. 22–23.

[5]*De Porphyrii studiis Homericis* (Göttingen 1853); accepted by K. F. Hermann. See "Classical Studies in America," 729; E. G. Sihler, "Klassische Studien und klassischer Unterricht in den Vereinigten Staaten," *Neue Jahrbücher für Pädagogik* 50 (1902) 506; W. M. Calder III, "Die Geschichte der klassischen Philologie in den Vereinigten Staaten," *Jahrbuch für Amerikastudien* 11 (1966) 217 ff. Calder, *Studies*, 19 ff.; W. R. Agard, "Classical Scholarship," in *American Scholarship in the Twentieth Century*, M. Curti, ed. (Cambridge, MA 1953) 147 ff.

[6]See O. Ribbeck, *Friedrich Ritschl* 2 (1881; reprint Osnabrück 1969) 279; W. Schmid, in *Wesen und Rang der Philologie: Zum Gedenken an Hermann Usener und Franz Bücheler* (Stuttgart 1969) viii; the same in *Bonner Gelehrte*, 135 with reference to F. Bücheler, *Kleine Schriften* 3 (Leipzig and Berlin 1930) 325, and ibid., 127 with reference to C. Jensen, "Das philologische Seminar von der Gründung der Universität bis zum Tode Jahns," in *Geschichte der Rheinischen Friedrich-Wilhelms-Universität zu Bonn* 2 (1933) 187 ff.; F. Ritschl, *Kleine philologische Schriften* 5 (Leipzig 1879) 33–39.

[7]E. G. Sihler, *From Maumee to Thames and Tiber. The Life-Story of an American Classical Scholar* (New York 1930) 101 f.; J. C. French, *A History of the University Founded by Johns Hopkins* (Baltimore 1946) 48, 430 f. In his "Address delivered before the American Whig and Cliosophic Societies of the College of New Jersey, at Princeton, June 20, 1877" (Princeton 1878), Gildersleeve passionately urged, in the full flush of the new foundation, the need for real university education in America.

[8]See P. Shorey, "Fifty Years of Classical Studies in America," *TAPA* 50 (1919) 42, and Gildersleeve, "Professorial Types," 13.

[9]See especially P. Shorey, "Basil L. Gildersleeve—1831–1924," *New York Times*, January 27, 1924, section 4, 3.

[10]J. A. Scott, *CP* 19 (1923–1924) 66; id., *CJ* 19 (1923–1924) 306–8; id., *PAPA* 56 (1925) xxii–xxviii (pp. xix–xxi are by C. W. E. Miller; see id., *Gildersleeve 6*, x); W. M. Thornton, "Gildersleeve, the Teacher," *University of Virginia Alumni Bulletin*, ser. 3

vol. 17 no. 2 (April 1924) 118-29; B. Sledd, "The Dead Grammarian," ibid., 134-36, "The Dead Grammarian," *New York Times*, January 11, 1924, 16; Th. Reinach, *Bull. de l'assoc. Guillaume Budé* 4 (July 1924) 39-45; G. Lodge, *CW* 17 (1923-1924) 113 f.; various addresses from the memorial meeting including one by Shorey in the *Johns Hopkins Alumni Magazine* 13,2 (January 1925) 121-48; C. W. E. Miller, *AJP* 45 (1924) 97-100. Professor Briggs adds: *Yearbook of the Poetry Society of South Carolina* (1924) 72; *The Confederate Veteran* 32 (March 1924) 104.

[11]E. G. Sihler (note 7 above) 101 ff., 254 f.; W. R. Agard (note 5 above) 148 f.; H. P. Houghton, "Gildersleeve on the First Nemean," *CJ* 49 (1953-1954) 215 ff.; H. T. Rowell, "Seventy-Five Years of the *American Journal of Philology*," *AJP* 75 (1954) 337 ff.; the editors, the *Johns Hopkins Magazine*, 9 (January 1958) cover and 1-2; R. J. Getty, "Bentley and Classical Scholarship in North America," *TAPA* 93 (1962) 34 ff.; W. M. Calder III (note 5 above) 218 ff. = *Studies*, 20 ff.; and in this volume, Kennedy. For dates of reprints, see Select Bibliography in this volume.

[12]W. M. Calder III, "B. L. Gildersleeve and Ulrich von Wilamowitz-Moellendorff: New Documents," *AJP* 99 (1978) 1-11 (=*Selected Correspondence*, 141-51); cf. "The Correspondence of Ulrich von Wilamowitz-Moellendorff with Edward Fitch," *HSCP* 83 (1979) 369-96 (=*Selected Correspondence*, 65-92).

[13]Idem, "Research Opportunities in the Modern History of Classical Scholarship," *CW* 74 (1980-1981) 249 = *Studies*, 11.

[14]Note 11 above.

[15]His fame grew the longer he lived, and by the time he reached 90 his birthdays were greeted with public fanfare. A biographer could not afford to overlook material in the press, since some of it is based on interviews. Clippings of numerous articles are to be found in the Baltimore archive.

[16]Professor Ward W. Briggs, Jr., has been vigorously researching these sources and has made some important discoveries whose publication is eagerly expected.

[17]The archivists are sorting the material generically: lectures, notebooks, offprints, etc., all stored in their own category. When I visited the archive any box might contain a variety of items (except for the correspondence, which has long been well organized). Thus the description here by category will correspond to the physical state of the archive. If anyone should wish detailed lists or more precise information than I give here, he is welcome to it *per litteras*. As this article goes to press, we learn that the cataloguing is all but complete.

[18]He would have come had the terms been better, indeed even reasonable.

[19]See W. M. Calder III, "Edward Capps," *DAB* Suppl. 4, 142-44.

[20]One letter, 4 December 1914, inviting Gildersleeve to speak at the organizational meeting of the Association of College Professors ("many of us regard you as the Doyen of American higher scholarship"); in refusing (5 February 1915, letter reprinted in *School and Society* [May 15, 1915] 717-18), Gildersleeve takes the opportunity to expatiate on the history of professorship in the United States. His remarks are taken almost verbatim from the first few pages of "Professorial Types."

[21]See below, pp. 75-76.

[22]See below, p. 75. These letters unfortunately contain nothing relevant to the matter discussed there.

[23]Kroll asks for a portrait of Gildersleeve for his seminar; Gildersleeve sends two; in the acknowledgment (21 October 1908) Kroll asks if he may keep one for himself, to hang in his study along with those of Mommsen, Diels, and A. Dieterich.

[24]One letter from Loeb (30 August 1910) requesting an opinion on his proposed series; in his (all but illegible) reply Gildersleeve is noncommittal and says that he once had the same idea himself and went so far as to approach a publisher, but that is as far as the idea went. Loeb also wrote to Wilamowitz with the same request; see W. M. Calder III, "Ulrich von Wilamowitz-Moellendorff to James Loeb: Two Unpublished Letters," *ICS* 2 (1977) 315-32 (=*Selected Correspondence*, 213-30).

[25]Apart from the letters in Sandys' own file, there is one quoted *in toto* by E. G. Sihler in a letter to Gildersleeve of 19 December 1903; and a letter from J. H. H. Schmidt to Sandys (4 September 1907; cf. Sandys' *History of Classical Scholarship* 3 [Cambridge 1921³] 158, n. 3) will be found in Schmidt's file. I suppose Sandys sent it to Gildersleeve.

[26]The author of the impossible metrical theory after Westphal and others that seduced not only Gildersleeve but Jebb and a good many more. Two long letters (30 May 1909, 8 June 1913) and one to Sandys (note 25 above) complain bitterly of his fate and rabidly denounce the German philological establishment, since no one believes his theories any more. A somewhat testy letter from Gildersleeve (18 June 1913) rebuts Schmidt's idea that Gildersleeve had betrayed him. In fact the American was so attached to the "old metrics" that he mourned their passing, even resented it, for the necessity of learning metre anew prevented him from completing his commentary on Pindar (see "Oscillations and Nutations," 47; *AJP* 26 [1905] 359 [=*Gildersleeve 6*, 119]; *AJP* 29 [1908] 368 ff. [=*Gildersleeve 6*, 166 ff.]; *AJP* 33 [1912] 233 [=*Gildersleeve 6*, 250]; *AJP* 34 [1913] 104 ff. [=*Gildersleeve 6*, 271 ff.]). He was too good a scholar not to realize that Wilamowitz and company had won the day. If he had not so liked the old theory he would have espoused the new, but as it was he merely withdrew plaintively from the field of battle. By contrast, Shorey raved against the new ideas in a series of articles that consistently missed the point while insisting that the other side had done so; see especially "The Issue in Metric," *CP* 19 (1924) 169-74; also "Word-Accent in Greek and Latin Verse," *CJ* 2 (1907) 219-24; "Choriambic Dimeter and the Rehabilitation of the Antispast," *TAPA* 38 (1907) 57-88; and various reviews: *CP* 13 (1918) 99 (Jebb's *Fragments of Sophocles*); 17 (1922) 150-53 (Wilamowitz's *Griechische Verskunst*); 19 (1924) 193 (Schroeder's *Pindars Pythien* and *Pindari Carmina*); 20 (1925) 342 (abstract of *Gnomon*).

[27]Son of F. W. Schneidewin. One letter, with a reply from Gildersleeve. Schneidewin had been visiting the States and took the opportunity to write his father's old pupil. The reply (25 March 1913) contains a quaint story. Gildersleeve remembers Göttingen with much fondness, and though Ritschl was his intellectual inspiration, Schneidewin was the teacher to whom he was closest (see "Professorial Types," 17). He writes to Max how well he remembers evenings at his father's home, and how on one occasion the young boy fell down the stairs. His father, fearing brain damage, leaned over him and inquired anxiously: "Max, lieber Max, was ist das Geschlecht von *ensis*?" When Max looked up and replied "masculini generis," his father beamed with relief.

[28]Numerous letters, including one of 28 February 1914, written after completion of his Berlin exchange professorship but before his departure from Germany. He describes his experiences at length, supplementing and to some extent contradicting his account at *CP* 24 (1929) 401-2. The letter includes remarks on the metrical controversy referred to above (note 26).

[29]See below, Part II.

[30]One letter from Wilson in his Princeton days, merely accepting an invitation.

[31]Gildersleeve's own adjective, *AJP* 31 (1910) 109 (=*Gildersleeve 6*, 196). See in this volume, E. C. Kopff, p. 57, and his remarks in "Wilamowitz and Classical Philology

in the United States of America: An Interpretation," read at the Wilamowitz conference in Bad Homburg, September 1981, and published in the proceedings of the same, *Wilamowitz nach 50 Jahren*, W. M. Calder III, H. Flashar, and Th. Lindken, eds. (Darmstadt 1985) 558-80.

[32]For some excerpts, see below, Part II. On Gildersleeve's lecturing style, see J. A. Scott in *PAPA* 56 (1925) xxii-xxviii, and W. M. Thornton (note 10 above); on the Harvard series, *AJP* 41 (1920) 93 (=*Gildersleeve 6*, 398). See also below, p. 74 (on the student's notebook).

[33]For further discussion of these lectures, see my "Gildersleeve's Pindaric Criticism," in *Greek Poetry and Philosophy: Studies in Honour of Leonard Woodbury*, D. E. Gerber, ed. (Chico 1984) 111-23.

[34]In a letter to Frank P. Brent of 27 October 1919, now in the possession of the University of Virginia, Gildersleeve states: "During my illness in 1916 my books and MSS were carted off to Homewood [a campus of J.H.U.] and I have never been strong enough since to reduce that chaos to order."

[35]On the other hand: "I have my notes [of Böckh] still; indeed, I have a whole shelf of notes on the lectures I heard in Germany. It is seldom visited" ("A Novice of 1850," 6). He refers to at least one visit to the shelf at "Oscillations and Nutations," 46.

[36]All the notebooks are labeled by the author. Where the year, semester, and location are not all given, the missing items can be deduced from the given ones or from the lecturer's name. Only two notebooks, those containing Böckh's lectures, date to 1850-1851 (the Berlin year); but the implication of the remarks at "A Novice of 1850," 6, is that Böckh's were the only lectures he attended that year. For Gildersleeve on his teachers, see *AJP* 5 (1884) 340; *AJP* 33 (1912) 233 (=*Gildersleeve 6*, 250); "Formative Influences," 615; "A Novice of 1850," 6 f.; "Professorial Types"; "Classical Studies in America," 728 ff. Further: on Leutsch, *AJP* 29 (1908) 373 (=*Gildersleeve 6*, 172); *AJP* 33 (1912) 233 (=*Gildersleeve 6*, 250); on Schneidewin, *AJP* 37 (1916) 373 (=*Gildersleeve 6*, 356 f.); on Bernays, *AJP* 32 (1911) 360 (=*Gildersleeve 6*, 231 f.); "Classics and Colleges," 72; "University Work in America," 108; *AJP* 28 (1907) 232 f. (=*Gildersleeve 6*, 142 f.); *AJP* 37 (1916) 242; *Gildersleeve 4*, 41 f.; "Oscillations and Nutations," 46 f.; on Ritschl, *PAPA* 9 (1876-1877) 14-15; *AJP* 5 (1884) 339-55; "Oscillations and Nutations," 48; on Franz, *Gildersleeve 4*, 33 f.; on Welcker, *AJP* 34 (1913) 232 (=*Gildersleeve 6*, 282). Other passing references are recorded in the exhaustive index to *Gildersleeve 6*.

[37]He also heard Immanuel Bekker in Berlin, but his lectures were deliberately incomprehensible, hence no notes; see *AJP* 28 (1907) 113 (=*Gildersleeve 6*, 141 f.). Franz's contribution to the young man's education was more in the way of *Übungen* than lectures: see "A Novice of 1850," 7.

[38]Page 1, i.e., about three-quarters of the way through the notebook, which also contains the lectures on Plautus.

[39]See "Classical Studies in America," 731 f.; *AJP* 5 (1884) 339; and see Ritschl's *Kleine Schriften* (note 6 above) vol. 5, pp. 1-18. By an ironic coincidence M. Gigante applies the same description, with equal accuracy, to Otto Jahn: *Parola del Passato* 29 (1974) 206.

[40]See A. Grafton's review of R. Pfeiffer, *A History of Classical Scholarship* 2 (1976) in *American Scholar* 48 (1979) 236-61; H. Lloyd-Jones in U. von Wilamowitz-Moellendorff, *History of Classical Scholarship*, tr. A. Harris (Baltimore 1982) xxix; M. Gigante (note 39 above) 196-224; R. Pfeiffer, *Philologia perennis* (*Festrede*, Bayer. Akad. d. Wiss., 3 Dec. 1960; München 1961).

[41]B. L. Gildersleeve, "The College in the Forties," *Princeton Alumni Weekly* 16 (June 26, 1916) 377-78; "Address delivered . . ." (note 7 above) 1 ff.

[42]See, e.g., "Formative Influences," 614.

[43]There is a fine translation into blank verse of Aeschylus *Agam.* 1-1177; cf. the translation of lines 367-474 in *New Eclectic* 6 (June 1870) 675-77, bearing the date November 1860. There is a translation also of Sophocles' *Electra*, and selections from Herodotus, Sophocles' *Ajax* and *OC*. On the latter see W. M. Thornton (note 10 above) 124.

[44]At least the pace suggested *prima facie* by the dates in the book: see below.

[45]"seem to be": see next paragraph.

[46]See "Pindaric Notes," *J.H.U. Circulars* (July 1916) 35: "the most characteristic and important part of [my] studies."

[47]Also to be found in this book (pp. 60-77, with the date of 7 December 1881) is a draft of "The Conditional Sentence in Pindar," *AJP* 3 (1884) 434-45.

[48]For the content, see my article, note 33 above.

[49]The notebook is titled "Unpublished Works. Study of Comparative Syntax. Preface dated April 15 [sic], 1882." This preface is published below in Part II.

[50]In "The Greek Seminary," *J.H.U. Circulars* (June 1910) 3-4, the order is: history, oratory, philosophy, comedy, other poetry. In *Syntax of Classical Greek* (=*Gildersleeve 3*) I, iv, we read: "Taking the Attic orators as the standard of conventional Greek, we have worked backward through philosophy and history to tragic, lyric, and epic poetry, comedy being the bridge which spans the syntax of the agora and the syntax of Parnassus." On "working backward," see below, p. 89 and note 155.

[51]A good deal of it eventually turns up as "Studies in Pindaric Syntax II, III," *AJP* 3 (1882) 446-55; 4 (1883) 158-65; and "On the Stylistic Effect of the Greek Participle," *AJP* 9 (1888) 137-57.

[52]*AJP* 28 (1907) 479 (=*Gildersleeve 6*, 149).

[53]See "Grammar and Aesthetics," 136: "Every one who has attempted the close grammatical study of a supreme work of art knows how hard it is to keep steadily at the task when the passion of the piece grows strong. The note-book ought to drop from the hand when Odysseus stands forth revealed. Then, like the hero, the reader strips off the rags of grammar and goes into the fight. But for all that the note-book should be picked up again and the patient assembly of facts resumed."

[54]*Gildersleeve 3*, I, iii.

[55]A letter to Henry Jackson of 28 March 1911 states explicitly what is only hinted at in the preface to Part II. By this time also Gildersleeve was over 80.

[56]*CP* 19 (1924) 307.

[57]*Gildersleeve 3*, I, iii.

[58]*AJP* 23 (1902) 1-27, 121-41, 241-60 (reprinted in booklet form, Baltimore 1903).

[59]*Southern Review* 1 (April 1867) 352-82 (=*Gildersleeve 2*, 161-205).

[60]Six popular articles on the Attic orators in the *Southern Magazine* for 1873: 12 (n.s. 5) 395-404, 559-69, 664-71; 13 (n.s. 6) 14-22, 129-37, 272-83; a series well worth reading. See in this volume, Kopff, p. 56.

[61]"Formative Influences," 613; "A Novice of 1850," 5; "Our Southern Colleges," *New Eclectic* 5 (Dec. 1869) 217 f. (the last item is not included in Miller's bibliography of Gildersleeve's works in *Gildersleeve 6*, xxx-liii).

[62]"Oscillations and Nutations," 48; see Sihler (note 7 above) 73.

[63]Certainly intentional.

[64]Portraits of Böckh are published by A. Gudeman, *Imagines philologorum* (Leipzig and Berlin 1911) 21; J. E. Sandys, *A History of Classical Scholarship* 3 (Cambridge 1921[3]) 96, and *A Short History of Classical Scholarship from the Sixth Century b.c. to the Present Day* (Cambridge 1915) 324; and E. Vogt, "Der Methodenstreit zwischen Hermann und Böckh und seine Bedeutung für die Geschichte der Philologie," in *Philologie und Hermeneutik im 19. Jahrhundert*, H. Flashar, K. Gründer, and A. Horstmann, eds. (Göttingen 1979), 103–21 (see p. 108).

[65]Possibly Charles Turner Torrey, abolitionist, executed at Baltimore in 1846 for helping slaves to escape (*DAB* XVIII, 595–96).

[66]*AJP* 28 (1907) 113 (=*Gildersleeve 6*, 142).

[67]See "A Novice of 1850"; "Formative Influences," 615.

[68]In the same book are found excerpts from letters home, 1850–1853; poems; and draft material for his novel (for which see below).

[69]Samuel Grant Oliphant (1864–1936). The *National Union Catalog* lists several unpublished works, mostly on educational topics, as well as a paper on "Magic and Folk-Lore in Plautus and Terence," presented to the Latin Seminar of J.H.U. in 1902, and his 1906 J.H.U. Ph.D. thesis, *A Study of the Vedic Dual Based upon the Rig-Veda and the Atharva-Veda* (Leipzig 1910). The thesis also appeared with a life appended as "The Vedic Dual: Part One. The Dual of Bodily Parts," *JAOS* 30 (1910) 155–85, which I have not seen. After graduating, Oliphant taught at Olivet College, Michigan.

[70]E.g., "Oscillations and Nutations," 49; *AJP* 23 (1902) 3; 37 (1916) 501 (=*Gildersleeve 6*, 372); "On the Present Aspect of Classical Study," *J.H.U. Circulars* (June 1886) 106 (=*Gildersleeve 2*, 506).

[71]See "Formative Influences," 615 f.

[72]W. M. Calder III (note 12 above, henceforth *Calder 1*) (=*Selected Correspondence*, 141–51); see also "The Correspondence of Ulrich von Wilamowitz-Moellendorff with Edward Fitch," *HSCP* 83 (1979) 369–96 (henceforth *Calder 2*) (=*Selected Correspondence*, 65–92).

[73]Various letters and documents yield dates of 1880, 1888, 1889, 1890, 1896, 1905, and one other of undetermined date between 1880 and 1888. (In 1889, however, he did not visit Germany.)

[74]See *AJP* 22 (1901) 229 (=*Gildersleeve 6*, 66).

[75]*Calder 1*, 9 (=*Selected Correspondence*, 149); cf. *Calder 2*, 379 (=ibid., 75).

[76]*Calder 2*, 379, n. 45 (=*Selected Correspondence*, 75, n. 45).

[77]Unpublished letter of 1 January 1907; Gildersleeve's reply the next day is the letter in *Calder 1*, 3 (=*Selected Correspondence*, 143).

[78]See Wilamowitz's letter to Fitch of 12 June 1907, *Calder 2*, 379 f. (=*Selected Correspondence*, 75 f.).

[79]Ibid., 379 (=75).

[80]Gildersleeve's letter to Fitch of 2 January 1907 (see note 77 above) refers to a letter he had received from Wilamowitz on the subject of Timotheus' *Persians*. Gildersleeve had presumably sent him a copy of his review of *Timotheos: Die Perser* (1903) in *AJP* 24 (1903) 222–36; cf. 110–11; an offprint, that is, or a complimentary copy of the *Journal*. In one of his letters to Fitch, Wilamowitz remarks that he had already seen Fitch's reviews in *AJP* for 1906, "da mir das Heft des Journal zugesandt war." Gildersleeve had naturally seen to it from the beginning that the *Journal* was sent to the most important European universities and, to judge from "mir," a few eminent individuals as well. How much of Gildersleeve's work Wilamowitz had actually read or heard of through his wife, who surveyed English scholarship for him (see W. M. Calder III, "Ul-

rich von Wilamowitz-Moellendorff to William Abbott Oldfather: Three Unpublished Letters," *CJ* 72 [1976-1977] 120), is unknowable, but he never mentions him in his scholarly work, only in his memoirs (*Erinnerungen*, 312). On the other hand, he knows the extent of Gildersleeve's contribution to philology and the general character of his work (*Calder 2*, 378 f. [=*Selected Correspondence*, 74 f.]); there must also be some substantive basis to the epithet "ehrwürdig," used already in 1906 (above). Another small item of information is that Wilamowitz knew that Gildersleeve had called him "imperious" in contrast with the "imperial" Böckh (*Erinnerungen*, 312). The place where Gildersleeve did this is "Oscillations and Nutations," 45, written in 1900 and published in the *J.H.U. Circulars* for April 1901. It seems certain that Gildersleeve sent Wilamowitz a copy of this at some time (it contains a warm appreciation of him); however, it seems equally certain that it was not sent until after they met. Wilamowitz would have acknowledged it, and Gildersleeve says in his letter to Fitch of 2 January 1907 (*Calder 1*, 3 [=*Selected Correspondence*, 143]) that he had only ever received one letter from Wilamowitz. (Calder's suggestion on this point, *Calder 1*, 10, n. 64 [=*Selected Correspondence*, 150, n. 64], seems to be made without knowledge of the passage in "Oscillations and Nutations.")

[81]See his letter below. See also Paul Shorey to Gildersleeve, 28 February 1914: "Wilamowitz spoke with great interest of you. He doesn't always agree with you but he evidently reads you — that is the advantage of being always readable." In *Pindaros* (Berlin 1922) there is no mention of Gildersleeve, but there is little mention of anybody.

[82]*Erinnerungen*, 312.

[83]*Calder 1*, 2 (=*Selected Correspondence*, 142). One is the letter on Timotheus (note 80 above); the other is an acknowledgment of Gildersleeve's "Notes on Stahl's Syntax of the Greek Verb," *AJP* 29 (1908) 257-79, 389-409; 30 (1909) 1-21; reprinted Baltimore 1909.

[84]*Calder 1*, 5 (=*Selected Correspondence*, 145). Wilamowitz's collection of offprints and working texts has recently been discovered in Berlin; the book may well be there, perhaps with marginalia.

[85]For Wilamowitz's correspondence, see W. M. Calder III, "*Doceat mortuus vivos*: In Quest of Ulrich von Wilamowitz-Moellendorff," *Emerita* 48 (1980) 215.

[86]Kurt Hildebrandt, "Hellas und Wilamowitz," *Jahrbuch für die geistige Bewegung* 1 (1910) 64-117; an abridgement is printed by G. P. Landmann, *Der George-Kreis: Eine Auswahl aus seinen Schriften*[2] (Stuttgart 1980) 141-49.

[87]"The Seventh Nemean Revisited," *AJP* 31 (1910) 125-53. See in this volume, Kopff, p. 59. In the letter of 30 October Gildersleeve had given fair warning of the coming disagreement. The offprint will be extant: note 84 above.

[88]"Pindars siebentes nemeisches Gedicht," *SPAW* Nr. 15 (1908) 328-52 (=*Pindaros und Bakchylides*, W. M. Calder III and J. Stern, eds. [*Wege der Forschung* 134, Darmstadt 1970] 127-58; =Wilamowitz, *Kleine Schriften*, 6 [Berlin 1935] 286-313).

[89]Calder customarily attaches significance to the absence of "College" for an American addressee (see, e.g., *Calder 2*, 373 [=*Selected Correspondence*, 69]) and is no doubt right to do so; but W. A. Oldfather is accorded the title, both in the appellation and the body of the letter (*CJ* 72 [1976-1977] 121, 125), so that Wilamowitz does not seem to have been consistent in this regard.

[90]See note 85 above.

[91]Possibly "ich nehme."

[92]See *Pindaros* (Berlin 1922) 491 on the opening of *Ol.* 1: "'Olympia ist das vornehmste Fest; das zu besingen bin ich zu Hieron gekommen.' Dies der einfache Gedanke, der durch den sprachlichen Schmuck geadelt wird." See further p. 310 on the

opening of *Isthm*. 2; pp. 387 f. and 392 on the narrative of *Pyth*. 4. The man, whether Pindar or Plato, was everything for Wilamowitz; one had to get at his mind by peeling away the layers of his art like so much clothing.

[93]A noteworthy and sincere statement, repeated in his letter to Fitch of 16 July 1921 (*Calder 2*, 389 [ = *Selected Correspondence*, 85]): "Wenn es Ihnen möglich ist, versichern Sie ihn meiner unveränderten Verehrung." For Gildersleeve's reaction to this letter, see below, p. 80.

[94]Hermann Collitz (1855–1935), Ph.D. Göttingen 1878. After a few years at Halle in not very satisfactory appointments (1883–1886), he emigrated to America where he taught first at Bryn Mawr College, and then from 1907 until his retirement in 1927 at J.H.U. See *Who Was Who in America*, 1 (Chicago 1943), s.v. He was primarily a Germanist but is best known to classical scholars as the editor with F. Bechtel et al. of the *Sammlung der griechischen Dialekt-Inschriften* (Göttingen 1884–1915). His papers are preserved at Baltimore and include a splendid store of Goethiana.

[95]At *AJP* 34 (1913) 487 ( = *Gildersleeve 6*, 295), after their meeting in any event, Gildersleeve is somewhat annoyed at the suggestion that Murray and Wilamowitz had penetrated Greek life to a degree not achieved by earlier generations—"to which I belong." But of course, Wilamowitz is not the one being blamed. For his admiration, see "Oscillations and Nutations," 50; *AJP* 23 (1902) 4; 24 (1903) 222; 37 (1916) 500 ( = *Gildersleeve 6*, 372) (quoting Murray); and in private places, the letter in *Calder 1* ( = *Selected Correspondence*, 141–51), and those to H. L. Ebeling published below.

[96]See Gildersleeve's obituary of Lane in *AJP* 18 (1897) 247.

[97]See *Gildersleeve 4*, 51: "Wilamowitz, the foremost Hellenist of our day."

[98]"Language" is crossed out and "idiom" written above the line. Apparently Gildersleeve does not wish to say outright that Americans, or perhaps only Harvard professors in 1911, would not understand the German.

[99]June 3 and 4, 1908: *"Greek Historical Writing" and "Apollo,"* tr. Gilbert Murray (Oxford 1908). In fact the lectures were read in Murray's translation (he spoke to the Philological Society in German): See W. M. Calder III, "Ulrich von Wilamowitz-Moellendorff on Sophocles: A Letter to Sir Herbert Warren," *CSCA* 12 (1979) 59, n. 29, and 60, n. 39. Gildersleeve must have assumed that the translations were made after the event.

[100]Wilamowitz lectured two evenings a week to halls packed not only with students but the socialites of Berlin: W. Jaeger, "Classical Philology at the University of Berlin 1870-1945," in *Five Essays*, tr. Adele M. Fiske (Montreal 1966) 58; Wilamowitz, *Erinnerungen*, 289 f.; J. Mejer, "Wilamowitz and Scandinavia: Friendship and Scholarship," in *Wilamowitz nach 50 Jahren* (note 31 above) 513-537 (see 524f.).

[101]There follows a paragraph of family matters. Harvard did ask Wilamowitz to come, but he declined (*Erinnerungen*, 290): "Dem Professorenaustausch mit Amerika habe ich ablehnend gegenübergestanden. Als ich von Harvard gewünscht ward, fragte das Ministerium daher nur telephonisch in einer Form an, der ich entnahm, man rechnete auf keine Zusage."

[102]"Oscillations and Nutations," 50, on the renewed call for training in verse composition: "At least the decree of Wilamowitz-Moellendorff has gone forth and there is nothing left for us oldsters, who have not stirred up the gift that is in us, except to plunge into the hiatus of one of Wilamowitz's own early pentameters. It is wide enough and deep enough, if I remember aright, to swallow up any devoted Curtius, hobby-horse and all." I have not located the guilty verse.

[103] "Oscillations and Nutations," 50; *AJP* 22 (1901) 232 (=*Gildersleeve 6*, 69); "Pindaric Notes," *J.H.U. Circulars* (July 1916) 36; and again in his response to the presentation of his *Festschrift*, printed in *Johns Hopkins University: Celebration of the Twenty-Fifth Anniversary of the Founding of the University and Inauguration of Ira Remsen, LL.D as President of the University* (Baltimore 1902) 162-64; p. 162: "One of the most dashing rough riders that have ever curveted on the plains of philology, or performed feats of lofty tumbling in the heights of scholarship. . . ." For further irreverence, see *AJP* 12 (1891) 387: "By the way, if any man desires to be avenged of a philological adversary he need only await Wilamowitz's leisure, for annihilation at his hands is merely a question of time. *Omnes eodem cogimur*"; and 16 (1895) 125 (=*Gildersleeve 6*, 31): "Such plain speaking helps to clear the philological air, even if some of us find the draught too strong, and close the windows hermetically with a shiver, as in a German lecture-room."

[104] P. 17a of the first "bundle" described above, p. 64. The reference seems to be to the fiery *Aus Kydathen* (Berlin 1880), although Gildersleeve may actually be thinking of the much more famous *Aristoteles und Athen* (Berlin 1893).

[105] The most vigorous assault on the Megarian tradition was delivered in an article in *Hermes* 9 (1875) 319-41, but the beginnings are in his doctoral dissertation, *Observationes criticae in comoediam graecam selectae* (1870) 1 ff.; see also his letter to Hermann Usener of 4 August 1873 in *Usener und Wilamowitz: Ein Briefwechsel 1870–1905*, H. Dieterich and F. Freiherr Hiller von Gaertringen, eds. (Leipzig 1934) 2 f. He retracted some thirty years later: *Kleine Schriften* (note 88 above) 5, 1.384; cf. *Erinnerungen*, 154, n. 2. See now Rudolf Kassel, *ZPE* 45 (1982) 283 ff., with corrections to the transcription of the letter to Usener at 283, n. 59.

[106] See note 102 above.

[107] What Gildersleeve found to be "truly German" about Wilamowitz's translations I do not know. Gildersleeve writes on them at *AJP* 13 (1892) 517 (=*Gildersleeve 6*, 15); cf. 20 (1899) 110 and 35 (1914) 368 (=*Gildersleeve 6*, 310). For a German's assessment, see Wolfgang Schadewaldt, *Antike Tragödie auf der modernen Bühne* (Heidelberg 1957) 51 (=*Hellas und Hesperien* 2[Zürich and Stuttgart 1970²] 636): ". . . ein seltsames Gemisch von Schiller, Geibel, protestantischem Kirchenlied, spätgoethischen Rhythmen, Hebbelschem Dialog mit seltsamen Abstürzen in den Alltagsjargon. . . ." For a hostile discussion of the translations, see K. Hildebrandt, "Hellas und Wilamowitz" (note 86 above). See also Wilamowitz, *Erinnerungen*, 254 ff.; H. Flashar, "Aufführungen von griechischen Dramen in der Übersetzung von Wilamowitz," in *Wilamowitz nach 50 Jahren* (note 31 above) 306-57.

[108] Gildersleeve uses the Kaiser's nickname again at "My Sixty Days in Greece," *Atlantic Monthly* 79 (1897) 206. Wilhelm's cousins gave it to him as a young man for his excitability; in later years it referred to his foreign policy. See Tyler Whittle, *The Last Kaiser* (London 1977) 60; in C. Burgauner's translation (1982), the German is "Wilhelm der plötzliche" — The passage is from "Harvard No. 1" (p. 64 above) 1898, 3.

[109] The passage is from the "first bundle" (p. 64 above) 21. See *Gildersleeve 4*, 27: some scholars "regard a Greek joke as a sacred thing, not lightly to be laughed at." For further remarks on German scholarship, see "Necessity of the Classics," *Southern Quarterly Review* 26 (July 1854) 157 ff., 162 (scorning the English, calling for scientific scholarship in America; on this youthful piece see *AJP* 36 [1915] 360 [=*Gildersleeve 6*, 335]; *AJP* 37 [1916] 496 [=*Gildersleeve 6*, 366 f.]); and *AJP* 38 (1917) 391-410 (in connection with Bywater). Whether treating Homer, Herodotus, Pindar, or Aristophanes,

Gildersleeve always showed himself immune to the grandiose theories of scholars; theories that never recommend themselves to those truly familiar with either literature or life. With the single exception of Schmidt's metrics, he never espoused any fashionable theory and so wrote much that is still fresh.

[110] The reference is to Wilamowitz's "Die griechische Literatur des Altertums," in *Die griechische und lateinische Literatur und Sprache*, U. von Wilamowitz-Moellendorff, Friedrich Leo, et al., eds. (*Die Kultur der Gegenwart* I 8, 1905) 107: "Das verbreitete Urteil ist, daß Polybios ein ausgezeichneter Historiker wäre, aber ein langweiliger Schriftsteller; viele sagen auch, ein kunstloser. Dies ist nun ganz verkehrt." Cf. *AJP* 31 (1910) 365 f. (=*Gildersleeve 6*, 208 f.).

[111]*Calder 2*, 379 (=*Selected Correspondence*, 75).

[112]Reading uncertain, possibly "altered."

[113]Johannes Vahlen (1830-1911); see Wilamowitz, *Kleine Schriften* (note 88 above) 6, 53-58; W. Jaeger, *Five Essays* (note 100 above) 49-50, 58.

[114]Especially *AJP* 22 (1901) 229 f. (=*Gildersleeve 6*, 66 f.); 24 (1903) 483 f. (=*Gildersleeve 6*, 106 f.); cf. 28 (1907) 233 f. (=*Gildersleeve 6*, 143 ff.); 33 (1912) 367.

[115]See the list of members in the appendix to Otto Ribbeck, *Friedrich Ritschl 2* (note 6 above).

[116]At *AJP* 22 (1901) 229 (=*Gildersleeve 6*, 66), Gildersleeve says he has "not exchanged a word" with Vahlen in all the years since they were students. Another letter from Vahlen is attested at *AJP* 38 (1917) 406; it is mentioned again and dated by Gildersleeve to "not long before his death" in a letter quoted in the Charleston *News and Courier*, 13 January 1924 (preserved in the Yates Snowden papers in the South Caroliniana Library, University of South Carolina).

[117]His European reputation is fairly represented by Gilbert Murray, "German Scholarship," *Quarterly Review* (April 1915) 333. If he wants advice on a technical point of grammar, says Murray, he goes to a German; but "supposing I wanted guidance on some very delicate point of Greek usage, and was looking for some one with a subtle *flair* and feeling for the language, there are two Americans and also certain English people whom I would consult in preference." (The other American is W. W. Goodwin.) Friedrich Blass declared himself "much delighted" with Gildersleeve's "splendid book," the *Syntax of Classical Greek*, and promised to write a review for the *Literarisches Centralblatt* (unpublished letter of T. D. Seymour to Gildersleeve, April 18, no year stated). (Blass was one of the few German scholars comfortable with English; he had written Seymour in that language.) Although Gildersleeve was wont to call himself a "humble syntactician" (e.g., *AJP* 14 [1893] 258), he was of course far more; but the only proper recognition of his true character by a European is, so far as I know, Theodor Reinach's obituary (note 10 above). However, one sometimes finds hints. J. E. Sandys, in preparing the Loeb edition of Pindar, ransacked *AJP* for Gildersleeve's *obiter dicta* (unpublished letter to Gildersleeve of 20 September 1914). Friedrich Leo was a keen follower of Brief Mention (unpublished letter of A. Gudeman to Gildersleeve, 16 April 1913). Writing from England to Gilman on 13 July 1905 about the conferral of honorary degrees at Cambridge and Oxford and the many kind things said about him in the proceedings, Gildersleeve refers to his edition of Pindar, "the thing that has made me more friends among English classical scholars than anything else I have done." Indeed, the conferral of those degrees amounts to considerable kudos. Gildersleeve complained from time to time about the European failure to recognize American scholarship; German ignorance would irritate more than English. In "Pindaric Notes," *J.H.U. Circulars* (July 1916) 35-37, he outlines the fortunes of his *Pindar* on the thirtieth anniversary of its publication;

at first it went unnoticed, but gradually acquired attention, especially with regard to his ideas about form and content, which he considered "the most characteristic and important part of [my] studies" (p. 35). At *AJP* 14 (1893) 501, Gildersleeve is heartened to see that Fennell has accepted his views on that topic. Wilhelm Christ, *Geschichte der griechischen Literatur* (Nördlingen 1888) 118, called Gildersleeve the "great American Pindarist"; in a notebook abstracting Christ's history, Gildersleeve has copied the phrase in capital letters. (The compliment is omitted in the third edition, 1898.)

[118]Although the fact that Vahlen never acknowledged them (note 116 above) rather makes against this. "iam pridem celebratum" need not be pressed; compliments and vituperation alike lose their edge in scholars' Latin.

[119]*AJP* 27 (1906) 102-3. See also his reviews of Usener's *Götternamen*, *AJP* 17 (1896) 356-66, and *Die Sintfluthsagen*, *AJP* 20 (1899) 210-15. For Usener, see further Franz Bücheler, *Neue Jahrbücher für das klassische Altertum, Geschichte und deutsche Literatur* 15 (1905) 737-42 (=*Kleine Schriften* vol. 3 [Leipzig 1930] 324-29) (= *Wesen und Rang der Philologie: Zum Gedenken an Hermann Usener und Franz Bücheler*, W. Schmid, ed. [Stuttgart 1969] 44-49); W. Schmid, ibid., v-x; A. Dieterich, *Archiv für Religionswissenschaft* 8 (1906) i-xi = *Kleine Schriften* (Leipzig and Berlin 1911) 354-62; Ed. Schwartz, *Gesammelte Schriften* 1 (Berlin 1938) 301-15; H. Herter in *Bonner Gelehrte*, 165 ff.; id., *Kleine Schriften* (München 1975) 655 ff.; H. J. Mette, "Nekrolog einer Epoche. Hermann Usener und seine Schule. Ein wirkungsgeschichtlicher Rückblick auf die Jahre 1856-1979," *Lustrum* 22 (1979-1980) 5-106.

[120]See W. Burkert, *Griechische Religion der archaischen und klassischen Epoche* (Stuttgart 1977) 23.

[121]Loc. cit., x. With less justice he adds "nicht bloß in Deutschland."

[122]20 September 1877; *Usener und Wilamowitz: Ein Briefwechsel 1870-1905* (note 105 above) 7. In Usener's letters below I have preserved his orthography.

[123]See above on Vahlen.

[124]*Götternamen* (Bonn 1896). A letter of 26 July 1896 among those in Bonn contains Gildersleeve's glowing appreciation of the book and his promise to review it (note 119 above).

[125]Usener envisaged further volumes on personification and metaphor but never found the time to write them.

[126]See *Usener und Wilamowitz* (note 122 above) 51 and n.

[127]Minton Warren (1850-1907), a member of the Bonn seminar and Gildersleeve's colleague in the chair of Latin; from 1899 he was professor at Harvard. See the obituary by K. F. Smith, *AJP* 28 (1907) 489. Gildersleeve's reply to this letter is one of the eight preserved in Bonn; he thanks Usener for his kindness, praises his work, and reports the progress of his own family.

[128]These sections deal with the "ellipsis of masculine substantives."

[129]Usener evidently did not find time since the review never appeared.

[130]Since 1896 Usener had had trouble with his eyes; see the correspondence with Wilamowitz (note 105 above) 57.

[131]"Eine Spur des Petrusevangeliums," *Kleine Schriften* 4 (Leipzig 1913; reprint Osnabrück 1965) 417-21.

[132]Albrecht Dieterich (1866-1908); see his *Kleine Schriften* (note 119 above) ix-xlii, and *Archiv für Religionswissenschaft* 11 (1907-1908) 161-62. Among the letters at Bonn is a brief, formal note of congratulation on the engagement, dated 6 November 1898.

[133]Usener forgets, Gildersleeve had only one.

[134]English punctuation is used nearly throughout; I have normalized to German.

[135]Of course he could have known, and nearly says as much in the draft but changed his mind, avoiding the admission that he had failed to acknowledge receipt. In a letter to G. M. Calhoun of 31 March 1913, he states: "As a rule I find it impossible for lack of time to acknowledge the receipt of books that are sent to me whether as an editor or as an individual." This subscription to *Rheinisches Museum* seems to be a personal one, and the reference to "giving a report" to apply to Usener's work however published; from the beginning reports of *Rheinisches Museum* had been made in the *Journal*, with one or two negligible hiatuses (twice written by Gildersleeve, *AJP* 21 [1900] 99–103, and 24 [1903] 349–52).

[136]A sentence has been omitted from the draft: "Obwohl ich von Ihren Verhältnissen nichts wusste, war ich im Begriff, durch das Journal die Aufmerksamkeit meiner Leser auf das Buch zu lenken—aber es hat mir an Zeit und Raum gefehlt." Actually he did know (note 132 above). The notice of Dieterich's book never appeared.

[137]For the Lanes, see above, p. 78.

[138]The draft has "emporgearbeitet," which would have been better.

[139]Usener did not in fact complete the second volume; Ludwig Radermacher published the first edition in 1904 (1929²).

[140]See "Classics and Colleges," 77; "University Work in America," 107.

[141]K. W. Krüger, *Griechische Sprachlehre für Schulen* (1875⁵).

[142]See "Formative Influences," 614; *AJP* 23 (1902) 3, 5.

[143]I.e., "paradigm."

[144]"the" written first.

[145]"aesthetic" added above the line.

[146]This word (or words) has so far completely eluded decipherment. See p. 70 above, 90 below.

[147]See "University Work in America," 101 f.

[148]See note 50 above.

[149]See *AJP* 23 (1902) 6: "For history we must have chronology and the various departments of Greek literature develop themselves chronologically, so that one important factor in the account is secure. But in the history of literature, chronology is not everything. The sphere must be considered, and the more one studies, the more one becomes convinced of the importance of the literary range. Each department of literature has a history of its own; each author has a stylistic syntax of his own; and these are the problems that have always interested me most, that have made of a passionate lover of literature a dispassionate dissector of language." Ibid., 258: ". . . my formulae are the results of a study of the living forces of language, and not mere convenient summaries of phenomena." Of the article from which these two quotations are taken Gildersleeve says in a letter to Shorey of 28 January 1911: ". . . my Problems of Greek Syntax, in which I have given what I consider the essence of my syntactical life." See further *PAPA* 24 (1893) xxvi: "In many of the dissertations that swarm over this field, history and chronology are treated as if they were practically identical, as if the emergence of a construction in literature were the emergence of the construction in language, and the disappearance of it from literature were its death. The individual counts everywhere, even if not so manifestly in Greek as in Latin; and in Greek the department is more potent than the individual. Take the familiar example of the articular infinitive. . . ." From a lecture, "Aristophanes" (p. 64 above: the lecture with a *t.p.q* of 1907) 13: "Historical syntax is often confounded with chronological syntax. In art the law of the genre is more potent

than the lapse of time, and when the individual has his rights, the sphere is very much circumscribed."

[150]We might say that language has synchronic states. Cf. the use of the word "crystallized" above.

[151]See "University Work in America," 106 f.; *PAPA* 24 (1893) xxv: "Hypotaxis is older than our record, and we cannot argue safely as to prehistoric processes with consciousness lost and analogy working its will; we cannot insist on the steadiness of the original function." The analogy of language to a biological organism is a commonplace of nineteenth century linguistic philosophy, originating in Goethe and Wilhelm von Humboldt; see the latter's *Schriften zur Sprache*, M. Böhler, ed. (Reclam, Stuttgart 1973) *passim*, with the editor's essay, 252 ff.

[152]See *AJP* 23 (1902) 5, 258; "University Work in America," 106 f.; "Grammar and Aesthetics," *passim*, especially 154–57; *Gildersleeve 4*, 74; obituaries by Gonzalez Lodge (note 10 above) and C. W. E. Miller (ibid.) 100; and "On the Present Aspect of Classical Study" (note 70 above) 506: "To me, as an ardent lover of literature, as one who was led through literature to grammar and not through grammar to literature, the fairest results of a long life of study have been the visions of that cosmic beauty, which reveals itself when the infinitely little fills up the wavering outline and the features stand out pure and perfect against the sky of God's truth."

[153]See "University Work in America," 121.

[154]It is revealing that Gildersleeve did not see much profit in the study of fragments, since one was hindered from seeing the beauty of the whole; J. A. Scott, *PAPA* 56 (1925) xxii.

[155]The lecture to college seniors (p. 64 above) 5, on the futility of harrowing the same old sorry bits of information to reconstruct the history of comedy; what is the point anyway, he asks, "[of] all this historical erudition . . . this lingering in the land of rudimentary efforts . . . to those who have yet to see the developed glory. For my part I cannot help expressing the opinion that there ought to be far more studying backward than there is, and a mastery of the organic connection can be attained just as well that way as in any other. Only it gives the teacher more trouble, just as a book of chronicles is easier to write than a history."

[156]In one of the lectures on Aristophanes (the same as in note 149) 13, he states the point clearly, briefly showing how each author entails special considerations: "The Holy Grail of Atticism is an elusive quest, and it is well that it should be so." No mention of inscriptions is made.

[157]See "University Work in America," 105.

This research was made possible by a General Research Grant from the Social Sciences and Humanities Research Council of Canada, administered by the University of Waterloo, for which I express my gratitude.

# EPILOGUE

Gildersleeve died in January 1924, in the 93rd year of his age. Cataracts had dimmed his sight in the later years, but his humor and intellect remained unimpaired to the end.

He was buried in University Cemetery in Charlottesville next to his two children who had died in infancy. He had announced his epitaph nine years earlier in a pamphlet circulated among his closest friends:[1]

> When my time comes, I will not say with Cassandra, ἀρκείτω βίος,[2] "Let life suffice," but with the unknown speaker of a fragment of Aeschylus, "Life's bivouac is o'er," διαπεφρούρηται βίος.[3] These words of a warrior remind me of Victor Hugo's "J'ai servi, j'ai veillé," "I have served, I have watched"—served as a teacher, watched as a critic; and of Landor's "warming both hands before the [bivouac] fire of life."[4] Διαπεφρούρηται βίος shall be my epitaph.

## NOTES

[1]"An Unspoken Farewell," (n.p. 1915), 4; see also his memorial notice of his great friend Emil Hübner, *AJP* 22 (1901), 114.

[2]Aes. *Ag.* 1314.

[3]Aesch. *Frag.* 265 (Nauck).

[4]"Dying Speech of an Old Philosopher":
I strove with none, for none was worth my strife:
Nature I loved, and, next to Nature, Art:
I warm'd both hands before the fire of life.
It sinks: and I am ready to depart.

# SELECT BIBLIOGRAPHY OF BASIL LANNEAU GILDERSLEEVE

*Gildersleeve 1* = *Pindar. The Olympian and Pythian Odes* (New York 1885; reprinted Amsterdam 1965).

*Gildersleeve 2* = *Essays and Studies, Educational and Literary* (Baltimore 1890; reprinted Minneapolis 1968).

*Educational Essays:*

| | |
|---|---|
| Limits of Culture | 3–40 |
| Classics and Colleges | 43–84 |
| University Work in America and Classical Philology | 87–123 |
| Grammar and Aesthetics | 127–157 |

*Literary and Historical Studies:*

| | |
|---|---|
| The Legend of Venus | 161–205 |
| Xanthippe and Socrates | 209–248 |
| Apollonius of Tyana | 251–296 |
| Lucian | 299–351 |
| The Emperor Julian | 355–398 |
| Platen's Poems | 401–450 |
| Maximilian; His Travels and His Tragedy | 453–496 |
| Occasional Addresses | 497–512 |

*Gildersleeve 3* = *Syntax of Classical Greek from Homer to Demosthenes*, with the co-operation of Charles William Emil Miller, 1–2 (New York 1900, 1911; reprinted with an *index locorum* by Peter Stork [Gröningen 1980]).

*Gildersleeve 4* = *Hellas and Hesperia, or the Vitality of Greek Studies in America* (New York 1909).

| | |
|---|---|
| The Channels of Life | 9–48 |
| Greek Language and Literature | 49–86 |
| Americanism and Hellenism | 87–130 |

*Gildersleeve 5* = *The Creed of the Old South, 1865–1915* (Baltimore 1915).

| | |
|---|---|
| The Creed of the Old South | 7–52 |
| A Southerner in the Peloponnesian War | 55–103 |

*Gildersleeve 6* = *Selections from the Brief Mention of Basil Lanneau Gildersleeve*, Charles William Emil Miller, ed. (Baltimore 1930).

Worthy of inclusion in this list, *honoris causa*, is *Studies in Honor of Basil L. Gildersleeve* (Baltimore 1902).

The dedication reads

To Basil Lanneau Gildersleeve, in commemoration of the seventieth anniversary of his birth, these studies are dedicated as a token of affection, gratitude, and esteem by his pupils.

For a full bibliography see *Gildersleeve 6*, xxx–liii.

# INDEX

Pearson, A.C., 64
Pinckney, Charles Cotesworth, 5
Pindar, 58, 64
  BLG's lectures on, 65
  Pindaric studies, 67–71
  suppressed preface on Pindaric syntax,
    86–89
  (*see also* BLG, *Publications: Pindar*)
Pitt Street, Charleston, 1
Plato
  "Ocean of the beautiful", 34
Platt, Arthur, 60
Poe, Edgar Allan, 9
Polybius, 80
Pound, Ezra, 57
Pratt, Johannah Frances Gildersleeve, 2
Pratt, Rev. Henry B., 2
Prentice, W.K., 64
Price, Thomas R., 16
*Princeton Review*, 44, 56
Princeton Seminary, 3
Princeton University, 9, 66, 73
Professional organizations
  drawbacks of, 30–31
Psalms, 3

**Q**

*Quarterly Review of Methodist Episcopal
Church*, 9

**R**

Radermacher, Ludwig, 82
Ramsay, David, 5
Rand, E.K., 64
Reinhold, Meyer, 29
*Rheinisches Museum*, 85
Ritschl, Friedrich, 9, 62, 65, 73, 80
  lectures on *Frogs*, Gk. comedy, "Kritik
    und Hermeneutik", Plautus, and
    "Encyclopädie der Philologie", 66
Robinson, D.M., 64
Robinson, W.J.N., 13
Rogers, George C., 5
Rowell, Henry T., 46, 48
Russell's Book Shop, Charleston, 5

**S**

Sandys, J.E., 64, 102
Savage, Arthur Duncan, 13
*Schlafhausen*, 9, 74
Schmidt, J.H.H., 64, 74
  BLG on metrical theory of, 95
Schneidewin, F.W., 9, 65
  lectures on Greek lyric poetry, 66
Schneidewin, Max, 64, 95
Schooler, Samuel, 13
Scott, J.A., 64, 71
Scott, Sir Walter, 5
  *Waverly Novels*, 3
Seymour, T.D., 64
Shakespeare, 3
Shilleto, Richard, 36
Shorey, Paul, 1, 64
  on BLG, 25, 48
Sihler, Ernest Gottlieb, 24, 64
Simms, William Gilmore, 4–6, 9
Smith, Charles Forster, 64
Smith, Kirby Flower, 64, 80
Smyth, H.W., 64
Sophocles, 52, 53
South
  and Greece, 4, 5
  antebellum, 4
*Southern Literary Messenger*, 9
*Southern Magazine*, 16
*Southern Review*, 16, 56
Sphacteria
  and Morris Island, SC, 5
Stork, Peter, 39
Stuart, D.C., 50, 51
Stuart, Gen. J.E.B., 14

**T**

*TAPA*, 37
Teuffel, W.S., 72
Thompson, John Reuben, 9
Thornton, William M., 13
Thucydides, 24, 47
  and the South, 51
  BLG's lectures on, 65
Ticknor, George, 22
Timrod, Henry, 5

Torrey, Charles Turner, 73
Tragedy
 BLG's lectures on, 74
 interest in after World Wars, 53
Trent, William P., 4, 56
Tyrtaeus, 16

**U**

Ullman, B.L., 64
University of Berlin, 23, 28
University of Bonn, 23, 28
University of California, 21
University of Göttingen, 23, 28, 62
University of the City of New York, 23
Usener, Hermann, 64, 81
 and BLG, 82
 letter to BLG, 82–83, 83–85
University of Virginia, 23, 62
 and Civil War, 14
 professorship of Greek, 9, 10

**V**

Vahlen, Johannes, 64
 and BLG, 80, 81

and Wilamowitzians, 81
 letter to BLG, 81
Van Hook, La Rue, 50, 51
Virgil, 5

**W**

Wackernagel, 36
Warren, Minton, 24, 83
Weil, Henri, 79
Welcker, F.G., 65
 lectures on Greek art, 66
Westminster Catechism, 6
Weyer's Cave, VA, 15
Wheeler, B.I., 64
White, Andrew D., 21
White, John Williams, 51, 64
Wilamowitz-Moellendorff, U. von, 25,
 48, 59, 64, 82, 92
 and BLG, 75–80
 at Oxford, 78
 *Herakles*, 51
 letter to BLG, 77
 "rough rider of classical philology", 79
Wilson, Woodrow, 64
Wolf, Friedrich August, 22, 66
Wolfe, Tom, 61